W9-CMA-961

"Nothing To Do But To Save Souls"

Books by Robert E. Coleman

Established by the Word
Introducing the Prayer Cell
Life in the Living Word
The Master Plan of Evangelism
The Spirit and the Word
Dry Bones Can Live Again
One Divine Moment (Editor)
Written in Blood
Evangelism in Perspective
They Meet the Master
The Mind of the Master
Songs of Heaven
Growing in the Word
The New Covenant
The Heartbeat of Evangelism
Evangelism on the Cutting Edge (Editor)
The Master Plan of Discipleship
The Spark That Ignites
Nothing to Do but to Save Souls
The Great Commission Lifestyle

"Nothing To Do But To Save Souls"

John Wesley's Charge to His Preachers

by Robert E. Coleman

FOREWORD BY DENNIS F. KINLAW

WESLEY HERITAGE PRESS
Box 7
Wilmore, Kentucky, 40394

Nothing to Do but to Save Souls
Copyright © 1990 by Robert E. Coleman
All rights reserved
Fourth Printing, 1994, U.S.A.
More than 45,000 copies in print

Library of Congress Cataloging in Publication Data

Coleman, Robert Emerson, 1928-
    "Nothing to do but to save souls": John Wesley's charge to his
preachers/by Robert E. Coleman; foreword by Dennis F. Kinlaw.
    p. cm.
    Includes bibliographical references.
    ISBN 0-915143-05-4 : $7.95
    1. Wesley, John, 1703-1791—Views on evangelistic work.
2. Methodist Church—clergy. 3. Methodist Church—Doctrines.
4. Clergy—Office. 5. Evangelistic work. 6. Salvation. 7. Holiness.
I. Title.
[BV3790.C57 1994]
287—dc20   993-50723

                                                              CIP

Wesley Heritage Press
Box 7
Wilmore, Kentucky 40390

Wesley Heritage Press is a ministry of the Francis Asbury Society.
The Press publishes books pertaining to the world-wide Wesleyan
Movement.

To
Frances Jean and Bob Sunderland
beloved friends
in the bonds of the Great Commission

Acknowledgments

Grateful acknowledgement is made to the following publications where portions of the material in this book originally appeared: to *Moody Monthly* for the article "Why Wesleyan Evangelism Worked" and an article "Wesley and Evangelism" in *Good News*, which contribute to the chapter "The Character of Wesleyan Evangelism"; to *The Preacher's Magazine* for the article "Do We Believe People are Lost?" from which comes some of the chapter "The Lostness of Mankind"; to *The Asbury Seminarian* for an article on justification, which largely comprises the chapter "The Just Shall Live By Faith"; and to *Good News* for the articles "What Does It Mean To Be Sanctified?" and "What Does it Mean To Be Holy?" constituting the chapter "The Mandate of Holiness."

Contents

Foreword   11

Introduction   15

1: **The Character of Wesleyan Evangelism**   25

2: **The Lostness of Mankind**   45

3: **The Just Shall Live by Faith**   61

4: **The Mandate of Holiness**   79

Epilogue   99

A charge to keep I have,
    A God to glorify,
A never-dying soul to save,
    And fit it for the sky.

To serve the present age,
    My calling to fulfill;
O may it all my powers engage
    To do my Master's will!

Arm me with jealous care,
    As in thy sight to live,
And O, thy servant, Lord, prepare,
    A strict account to give.

Help me to watch and pray,
    And on thyself rely,
Assured, if I my trust betray,
    I shall forever die.

—Charles Wesley

Foreword

One of God's greatest gifts to His children is the prophet. We are so easily misled by the wisdom of the day and the worldly-wise. We need someone with the longer look who can save us from the blindness of our immediacies and the folly of our superficial understandings. We see so easily what seems to be rather than what really is. That is why we are so perpetually wrong about what is to be.

Our world is like an orchard so full of beauty and promise but also touched by blight. Many of the greatest trees, once fruitful, are now barren and dead. Workers tend the untouched trees, busily pruning, digging, fertilizing. We encourage them in their labors because the fruit is so vital to our lives. We seem not to notice that some of the trees most aggressively tended are among the first to die. The workers are sincere, work so hard, and have the approval of so many of their superiors. It would be unthinkable to us that there could be a relationship of death and not of life between their activity and the health of the trees. After all, the results are not instant. Then comes the prophet.

It is seldom that a prophet is popular. His point of view is so contradictory to the common wisdom. Worse, his influence often becomes disruptive to established procedures. He can be seen as a threat to the structures. His only allies are time, the quickened conscience, the Spirit-touched understanding, and history. Little wonder that he is seen as "a troubler of Israel" and must be, for comfort's sake, neutralized.

Robert Coleman in this little volume is a prophet. He sees the obvious and that takes some doing. The reality is that it takes the divine touch. Coleman knows his Bible. He knows the history of his church. He loves both. His concern is the obvious malaise in the church, which he owns.

Some will call Coleman an obscurantist. The charge will be false. He speaks from our past. But that past is not dead. It is more alive than we are. As one wiser than I said, our past is the only part of us that is really alive. One of the evidences of our malaise is our understanding of the importance of a person's past in bringing the person to psychic health while we deliberately cut ourselves off from our Christian history. Coleman speaks to us from our past and that is not obscurantism.

Others will say he is a pessimist. That charge too will be wrong. The book pulses with hope. The reason is that he speaks from the future—a future that is as real as the promise of Jesus of Nazareth is true. After all, Jesus did not say our institutions would prevail but that the kingdom would. And the two are not identical. If the institution that Coleman loves so much could hear what he has to say, the contrast between the two would be far smaller.

One of the beautiful things about this little book is that it sings. I recommend that, if possible, you read it at a sitting. If you read it piecemeal, you may miss the song. It is not surprising though that it sings. Most true prophets do. When a mortal is touched by the divine hand so that he can see beyond the flux and ambiguities of time to the glory of the Eternal, he usually sings. That is why a biblical prophet is usually a poet.

It normally takes the people of God time to recognize when a prophet has been among them. We may be like our fathers in this. That will be our loss, loss for the church and for the world. That loss will not change the fact that a prophet has spoken. God gives gifts to the church, and He has given again.

Dennis F. Kinlaw, President
Asbury College
Wilmore, Kentucky

Introduction

THE WONDER OF THE GOSPEL WITNESS

An overwhelming wonder fills my soul when I think of the redeeming grace of God—a sense of amazement that grows with the years. My feeling is expressed aptly by Charles Wesley in one of his hymns.

> And can it be that I should gain
> An interest in the Savior's blood?
> Died He for me, who caused His pain?
> For me, who Him to death pursued?
> Amazing love! how can it be
> That thou, my Lord, shouldst die for me?[1]

Such love "surpasses knowledge" (Eph. 3:19, NIV). I can understand God condemning me for my iniquity, for He is holy. And I can comprehend God sentencing me to death, for He is just. But for Him to accept my judgment Himself—to give the incarnate Son to die in my place—is too wonderful for my finite mind to grasp. In contemplating it, all I can do is fall at His feet and exclaim:

> 'Tis mercy all, immense and free!
> For O my God! it found out me![2]

The realization of this amazing grace, with its resulting worship of the Lamb, creates a desire to mount every housetop and proclaim God's good news to a lost world. Herein is the compulsion of evangelism. A sense of human need may move us to care, and duty may call us to get

involved, but supremely it is the adoring love of Jesus that
makes us evangels of the Gospel.

THE PRIORITY OF MINISTRY

A church full of the Holy Spirit lives in this devotion.
Christian witness has many aspects, of course, but evangelism is the cutting edge. Indeed, it brings the church into
existence, for apart from introducing sinners to the Savior
there would be no fellowship of believers. That is why
Wesley's charge to his preachers rings so true to the
priorities of the kingdom:

> It is not your business to preach so many times,
> and to take care of this or that society; but to save
> as many souls as you can; to bring as many sinners
> as you possibly can to repentance, and with all your
> power to build them up in that holiness without
> which they cannot see the Lord.[3]

The admonition only echoes the command of Christ to
his disciples when he commissioned them to "go and
disciple all nations" (Matt. 28:19). Though this directive
may be obscured today by many other activities occupying
attention, it was the heartbeat of Methodism during the
formulative years of the movement. Interestingly, in the
present "Historical Statement" of the official *Discipline*,
this controlling purpose is still affirmed as "the only
infallible proof of a true church of Christ."[4]

A PASSION FOR SOULS

One does not have to read long in the accounts of the
pioneer Methodists to recognize their passion for souls.
Freeborn Garrettson, a minister of the church, illustrates
something of this dedication when he spoke to the New
York Conference early in the nineteenth century.

> I traversed the mountains and valleys, frequently
> on foot, with my knapsack on my back, guided by
> Indian paths in the wilderness, when it was not

expedient to take a horse. I had often to ride through morasses, half deep in mud and water; frequently satisfying my hunger with a piece of bread and pork from my knapsack, quenching my thirst from a brook, and resting my weary limbs on the leaves of trees. Thanks be to God! He compensated me for my toil; for many precious souls were awakened and converted to God.[5]

Turn almost any place in John Wesley's Journal and this same passion for evangelism comes through. Take, as an example, the evening of May 13, 1740, when he preached at Upton, a little town near Bristol. "I . . . offered to all those who had ears to hear, 'repentance and remission of sins,'" he said. "The devil knew his kingdom shook, and therefore stirred up his servants to ring bells, and make all the noise they could." But not to be outdone, Wesley increased the intensity of his appeal, until his ". . . voice prevailed so that most of those that were present heard 'the word which is able to save their souls.'"[6]

To save souls! That was the mission of the Word— the preeminent reason for God giving us a revelation of His grace. The Word can never be divorced from the mission without losing its purpose. Nor can the mission be separated from the message without losing its power. Early Wesleyans kept the two together.

MISSIONARY EVANGELISM

Out of such flaming zeal for souls emerged a missionary church in the new world. Moreover, to a remarkable degree, Methodists maintained this evangelistic focus well into the nineteenth century. Francis Asbury, after forty-five years of labor, wrote in 1815:

The Methodist preachers, who had been sent by John Wesley to America, came as missionaries . . . And now, behold the consequences of this mission. We have seven hundred travelling preachers, and three thousand local preachers, who cost us noth-

ing. We will not give up the cause—we will not
abandon the world to infidels.[7]

Typical of those preachers was Thomas Ware, whose
ministry began in 1775. One day he was asked by a clerical
opponent whether he was a missionary. "I replied," he
said, "that I am a Methodist, and we were all missionaries."[8]

So pervasive was this spirit that the terms "preacher"
and "missionary" seem to have been used interchangeably.
For example, Abel Stevens in characterizing the work of
John Major, who died in 1788, refers to him as being
moved by Christ's passion for the lost, "one of the earliest
missionaries of the Methodist Episcopal Church in Geor-
gia."[9] Jesse Lee, a pioneer Methodist itinerant, speaks of
several preachers "locating," among them James Haw "the
first missionary to Kentucky, who had been travelling ten
years."[10] John Kobler says that he "was sent by Bishop
Asbury as a missionary to the North Western Territory" in
order "to plant the first principles of the Gospel."[11]

Persons outside the official structure commonly referred to the circuit riders in identical terms. The experience of a Presbyterian traveler during this period would not
be strange when he observed:

> I at length became ambitious to find a family whose
> cabin had not been entered by a Methodist
> preacher. In several days I traveled from settlement
> to settlement on my errand of good but into every
> home I entered I learned that the Methodist
> missionary had been there before me.[12]

EXTRAORDINARY GROWTH

Clearly American Methodism was conceived as a
missionary movement, calculated to win the greatest
number of people in the shortest possible time. And, as no
other fellowship in Western Christianity, they did just that.
Within one generation this fledgling sect, after its formal
organization in 1784, grew from a few thousand adherents

to the largest denomination in the land. It surpassed in size its nearest rival, the Baptists, by twenty percent; and numbered as many members as all Episcopalians, Congregationalists, and Presbyterians combined. Astounding! About fifty years from the time the first Methodists set foot on these shores, more than a quarter of all professing Christians in America, Protestant or Catholic, belonged to the Methodist Episcopal Church.[13] Had the rate of increase continued for a few more generations, every man, woman, and child on the continent would have been won to Christ and called a Methodist!

As the years lengthened, however, the evangelistic momentum subsided, and by the turn of the twentieth century decline of church growth was clearly evident, a trend that has drastically accelerated in recent years. Much of the Methodist membership loss has been amalgamated into other branches of the Christian family where a more hospitable evangelical environment now exists. We can be grateful for the way former Methodists have enriched the ministry of other churches, even as they have added to their numbers. But one cannot help but have a certain nostalgia for those early days when Methodism was probably the greatest soul-saving movement on the face of the earth.

REASONS FOR GROWTH

Historians and missiologists continue to speculate as to reasons for this amazing chapter in American church growth.[14] Doubtless the way Methodism was organized was a factor. Controlled by a missionary vision, its structures developed with keen sensitivity to the needs of an unsophisticated and largely scattered society. The itineracy was a reflection of this concern; it enabled their preachers to move quickly into targeted areas of unreached people. Also, the church was mobile and flexible enough to permit rapid distribution of manpower, while at the same time sufficiently centralized through the Conference system to assure maximum administrative efficiency.

The disadvantages of the traveling ministry were offset by the organization of the local societies into bands, classes, and meetings of various kinds, cared for by their own lay leaders. Within the fellowship of these close-knit communities of faith, they ministered to one another in love. Each member found an unprecedented opportunity for spiritual and social development. For the first hundred years of Methodism it would be hard to find in Christendom a more effective system of discipleship.

Reinforcing this facility of mutual oversight was a methodical discipline for which in derision they were originally named. Method-ists had to measure up to standards of conduct becoming their Lord, an expectation fostered through all their avenues of learning. Though there was little interest in higher education, no church was more involved in lay training and the instruction of children in Sunday schools. Mention also must be given to the Book Concern, established in 1789 and eminently successful in disseminating Christian literature.

In terms of experience, heartfelt religion was the normal temper of the denomination, and its patterns of worship, preaching, and singing were geared to this impulse. Their practices were especially attractive to the socially oppressed and emotionally starved masses. Here the poor could feel at home. Even large numbers of slaves, a group largely ignored in early America, found in the Wesleyan societies a haven of rest.

Above all, undergirding the Wesleyan way of life and constraining their outreach was a simple faith in the Gospel of salvation. Apart from this affirmation of the soul, other considerations of church growth would be as sounding brass and a tinkling cymbal. Strangely, though, theology is an area often overlooked or passed over casually within Methodist circles in contemporary discussions of evangelism and church expansion.

FOCUS OF THE BOOK

This collection of essays speaks to this issue of experiential faith. As such, it is not another book on general church-growth theory.[15] Though mindful of the extensive body of behavioral research into what makes churches grow or decline, the concern of this book is upon deeper spiritual realities—those convictions of the heart that engender and sustain dynamic evangelism.

The focus is upon Wesleyan thought and commitment, with no sectarian intent of belittling other evangelical systems of doctrine. It simply happens that I have grown up and ministered within the Methodist connection, and I understand its strengths and weaknesses better than those of other communions. However, what is presented in reference to my own heritage, in so far as it truly interprets scriptural verities, applies to evangelism in any context.

Even here the approach is very selective. Beginning with the conversion of John Wesley, some significant aspects of evangelism in Methodist experience are noted. At this point, attention turns to the anguishing question of judgment and the necessity of reaching the lost. I move then to the promise of justification by faith in Christ and regeneration of life through the Holy Spirit. With this in view, I consider the ever-expanding possibilities of sanctification and its witness of love to the world, clothing evangelism with the beauty of holiness. Appropriate to this message, the book concludes with a call to faithfulness in the true succession of our forefathers.

NEED FOR LEADERSHIP

It is my hope that looking again at the roots of Wesleyan evangelism, though it be but a brief glimpse, will bring us to see anew that deep conviction of truth which drove our forefathers to proclaim the Gospel and invite "whosoever will" to come to Christ. I think that all of us could well afford to spend some time reviewing the values that thrust us forth in ministry.

A few months before Wesley died on March 2, 1791, the last entry in his Journal noted that he had exhorted a large congregation in Spitalfields to "put on the whole armor of God." Then in the afternoon, to a still more crowded church at Shadwell, he recorded that he spoke on the text, "One thing is needful," adding the comment, "and I hope many, even then, resolved to choose the better part."[16]

This is the obsession bequeathed to us—the burning desire that every person yield himself fully to the claims of Christ. As you read here what this commitment meant to the first Methodists, may something of that same compulsion be felt to "put on the whole armor of God," and so to "choose the better part."

NOTES

[1]Charles Wesley's hymn, *And Can It Be that I Should Gain.*
[2]Ibid.
[3]John Wesley, included in the *Minutes of Several Conversations Between the Rev. Thomas Coke, LL.D., the Rev. Francis Asbury, and Others, at a Conference Begun in Baltimore . . . in the year 1784, Composing a Form of Discipline for the Minister, Preacher, and Other Members of the Methodist Episcopal Church in America* (Philadelphia: Charles Cist, 1785), 12. These *Conversations* became the first *Discipline* of the Methodist Episcopal Church.
[4]The statement reads: "The United Methodist Church believes today, as Methodism has from the first, that the only infallible proof of a true church of Christ is its ability to seek and to save the lost, to disseminate the Pentecostal spirit and life, to spread scriptural holiness, and to transform all peoples and nations through the Gospel of Christ," *The Book of Discipline of the United Methodist Church* (Nashville: The United Methodist Publishing House, 1988), 10.
[5]Quoted by Halford E. Luccock and Paul Hutchinson, *The Story of Methodism* (Nashville: Abingdon-Cokesbury, 1926), 230.
[6]John Wesley, *The Journal of the Rev. John Wesley*, ed. Nehemiah Curnock, 8 vols. (London: Epworth, 1909), 2:346. John's letter to his brother Charles on April 26, 1772, sums up his thinking: "Your business as well as mine is to save souls. When we took Priest's orders, we undertook to make it our business. I think every day lost which is not (mainly at least) employed in this thing," *The Letters of the Rev. John Wesley*, ed. John Telford, 8 vols. (London: Epworth, 1931), 5:316.
[7]Francis Asbury, *The Journal and Letters of Francis Asbury*, ed. Elmer T. Clark, 3 vols. (Nashville: Abingdon, 1958), 2:787.
[8]Thomas Ware, *Sketches of the Life and Travels of Rev. Thomas Ware* (New York: Lane & Sandford, 1842), 263, 189.
[9]Abel Stevens, *History of the Methodist Episcopal Church*, 4 vols. (New York: Eaton and Mains, 1867), 2:49–50.

[10] Jesse Lee, *A Short History of Methodists in the United States of America, Beginning in 1776, and Continuing Till 1809* (Baltimore: Magill and Cline, 1810), 166.

[11] Quoted by J. B. Finley, *Sketches of Western Methodism: Biographical, Historical, and Miscellaneous*, ed. W. P. Strickland (Cincinnati: Methodist Book Concern, 1855), 169.

[12] Walter Brownlow Posey, *Frontier Mission* (Lexington, KY: University of Kentucky Press, 1966), 19.

[13] The percentage of Methodist Christians to the total church population in America continued at about this same ratio until near the end of the nineteenth century, though the evangelistic momentum of the church began to decline several decades earlier. Church membership estimates upon which these generalizations are based should not be taken as definitive, though an effort has been made to interpret fairly the limited information available for this period. For a comparative chart on the statistical progress of American Methodism, see Robert Coleman, "Is Methodism Growing or Just Keeping Up?" *District Evangelism*, I:4 (Nashville: Board of Evangelism, United Methodist Church, 1955), 2; cf. Daniel Dorchester, *The Problem of Religious Progress* (New York: Phillips and Hunt, 1895), 446, 537–38; H. K. Carroll, *The Religious Forces of the United States* (New York, 1893); W. W. Sweet, *Religion in Colonial America* (New York, 1951), 271f., 334–36; W. S. Salisbury, *Religion in America* (New York, 1951); Benson Y. Landis, *Religion in the United States* (New York, 1965). More recent denominational statistics may be found in the annual *Yearbook of American & Canadian Churches*.

[14] Many American Methodist historians, like Jesse Lee, Nathan Bangs, Abel Stevens, James M. Buckley, and William Warren Sweet, explain the growth primarily in terms of an "ingenious church polity and a democratic theology," as noted by Kenneth E. Rowe in his essay "Counting Converts: Progress Reports as Church History," *Rethinking Methodist History*, ed. Russell E. Richey and Kenneth E. Rowe (Nashville: Kingswood Books, 1985), 11–17. The feeling by these historians seems to be that the best religion spreads the fastest, an assumption that, I think, may be open to question. But, at least, it is a factor that cannot be overlooked in considering the vitality of a church. An explanation of Methodist growth primarily from the standpoint of church polity and methodology is the recent book by George G. Hunter III, *To Spread the Power* (Nashville: Abingdon, 1987). For a contemporary general review of Methodism in this country, see Frederick A. Norwood, *The Story of American Methodism: A History of the United Methodists and Their Relations* (Nashville: Abingdon, 1974); or the works of Frank Baker, Stanley J. Menking, Emory S. Bucke, or John G. McEllhenney. A basic bibliographic listing of materials in the larger context of Wesleyan study is compiled and edited by Kenneth E. Rowe, *United Methodist Studies* (Nashville: Abingdon, 1987).

[15]For a comprehensive overview of the modern church-growth movement, including a glossary of terms and with presentations from representative leaders, see *Church Growth: State of the Art,* ed. C. Peter Wagner, with Win Arn and Elmer Towns (Wheaton: Tyndale, 1986). A representative bibliography of literature related to the discipline will be found in *The Complete Book of Church Growth,* eds. Elmer L. Towns, John N. Vaughan, and David J. Seifert, 2d ed. (Wheaton: Tyndale, 1985), 388–94.

[16]Wesley, *Journal,* 8:110.

CHAPTER ONE

The Character of Wesleyan Evangelism

BIRTH OF METHODISM

You are in London on a September Sunday afternoon in 1739. Having sought to find the place of greatest excitement, you have gone to Moorfields to join the throng milling about on Kennington Common. By their poor dress and crude manners, you recognize that most of the people are of the common sort. Not a few of them appear disinterested, even riotous on the fringe of the crowd. But as you slowly work your way through the uncultured multitude and into the inner circle, you notice the attention of onlookers change. Idle chatter gradually gives way to respectful silence. You see tears coursing down the grimy faces of stalwart men and resolute women as they listen intently to an unstrained voice coming from the center of the gathering.

It takes you a moment to distinguish the speaker, for he stands scarcely five feet four inches tall. Pushing forward a bit more and standing on tiptoe to get a better view, you see a man wearing the clerical garb of an Anglican priest. Long silken hair falls upon his shoulders. His eyes flash with conviction as he lifts his arm and in clear, resonant tones, repeats, "Believe on the Lord Jesus

Christ, and thou shalt be saved."[1] You may not know that
you are in the presence of John Wesley, the most influential
leader of the eighteenth-century spiritual awakening.

Forces for renewal set in motion through his life and
work still reverberate around the world. At the heart of this
amazing influence, giving direction and urgency to the
whole, was a determination to make Christian disciples.
While we live in a different age, some characteristics of his
evangelism are as relevant today as ever.

THE OVERFLOW OF
CHRISTIAN EXPERIENCE

For Wesley, Gospel witnessing issues from experiential knowledge of our living Lord and Savior. This may be
seen in his own search for personal faith, which, after a
long and sometimes agonizing quest, climaxed at a small
Moravian chapel on May 24, 1738. Waking early that
morning, he read in his New Testament, "Whereby are
given unto us exceeding great and precious promises; that
by these ye might be partakers of the divine nature"
(2 Peter 1:4). Then he opened his Bible again. This time
his eyes fell on the words of Jesus: "Thou art not far from
the kingdom of God" (Mark 12:34). All morning these
promises kept running through his mind.

In the afternoon he went to stately St. Paul's Cathe-
dral, where he was especially moved by the choir's singing
of Psalm 130: "Out of the deep have I called unto thee, O
Lord; Lord, hear my voice." The final verses seemed to
stir his soul: "O Israel, trust in the Lord; for with the Lord
there is mercy, and with him is plenteous redemption. And
he shall deliver Israel from all her sins."

These words were still echoing in his mind as he made
his way to the little meeting on Aldersgate Street. We are
not told how the service progressed, though it is known
that the lesson that evening spoke of the transformation
resulting from the new birth. As the young clergyman
listened, about a quarter before nine, something happened.
He explained it this way:

While he was describing the change which God works in the heart through faith in Christ, I felt my heart strangely warmed. I felt I did trust in Christ, Christ alone for salvation; and an assurance was given me, that he had taken away my sins, even mine, and saved me from the law of sin and death.[2]

Note what instinctively followed. Wesley said: "I began to pray with all my might for those who had in a more special manner despitefully used me and persecuted me." What began as an inward experience of salvation now found immediate expression in a constraint to pray for others, an impulse that erupted in personal witness, as he added, "I then testified openly to all these what I now first felt in my heart."[3]

Having witnessed to those present, John Wesley, with some friends, went immediately to tell the good news to his brother Charles, who lay sick in a house nearby. Rushing into his room, John exclaimed, "I believe!" Then, typifying their unbounded joy, they joined in singing a hymn that Charles had composed following his own conversion three days before:

Where shall my wondering soul begin?
How shall I all to heaven aspire?
A slave redeemed from death and sin,
A brand plucked from eternal fire,
How shall I equal triumphs raise,
Or sing my great Deliverer's praise?

O how shall I the goodness tell,
Father, which thou to me hast showed:
That I, a child of wrath and hell,
I should be called a child of God,
Should know, should feel my sins forgiven,
Blest with this antepast of heaven!

And shall I slight my Father's love?
Or basely fear His gifts to own?
Unmindful of His favors prove?
Shall I, the hallowed cross to shun,

Refuse His righteousness t'impart,
By hiding it within my heart?

Outcasts of men, to you I call,
Harlots and publicans and thieves!
He spreads His arms t'embrace you all;
Sinners alone His grace receive.
No need of Him the righteous have;
He came the lost to seek and save.

Come, O my guilty brethren, come,
Groaning beneath your load of sin!
His bleeding heart shall make you room;
His open side shall take you in.
He calls you now, invites you home:
Come, O my guilty brethren, come![4]

From such heartfelt assurance Methodism was born.
It was believed that one could know for certain a relationship with God, as Wesley explained in one of his sermons:

> The Spirit of God . . . so works upon the soul by
> his immediate influence, and by a strong, though
> inexplicable operation, that the stormy wind and
> troubled waves subside, and there is a sweet calm;
> the heart resting in the arms of Jesus, and the
> sinner being clearly satisfied that God is reconciled,
> that all his iniquities are forgiven, and his sins
> covered.[5]

This truth pertained whether speaking of justification
or the inner working of the Spirit in sanctification.
Whatever the promise of redeeming grace, it could be
realized by faith, and that without delay. Little wonder
someone observed that Methodist homes could be iden-
tified by the sound of singing. They were enjoying the
fruits of salvation, and in that assurance the glad tidings
could not be self-contained.

Only in the same way, can evangelism be sustained
today. The Gospel must become in us like a living spring of
water if it is to flow forth to thirsty souls. Too often we

have tried to work it up by well-intended exhortations or expertly designed programs. But there is no action of love because there is no "strangely warmed" heart. The first requirement of real evangelism is an authentic, up-to-date, joyous, Spirit-endued experience with the crucified and risen Christ.

SPIRITUAL AUTHORITY

Keeping this witness on course, Wesley's message always moved within the context of biblical truth. The Scriptures had become central in his thinking even before his conversion. In fact, they were instrumental in bringing him to know salvation. While at Oxford, with others in the Holy Club, he had resolved to take the Bible as "their whole and sole rule," it being "their one desire and design to be downright Bible-Christians."[6]

Thereafter, this determination permeated his whole ministry, as is evident from the constant appeal to Scripture in his writing and preaching. "The Bible is my standard of language as well as sentiment," he said.[7] Scripture, to him, was "the only standard of truth, and the only model of pure religion."[8] Endeavoring to live by this rule, Wesley resolved to be "a man of one book. Yes, I am a Bible bigot," he asserted. "I follow it in all things, both great and small."[9]

His practice was the reflection of a conviction that the Bible was fully inspired by God. Biblical passages were often referred to as the very words of the Holy Spirit.[10] Therefore, according to Wesley, "nothing which is written therein can be censured or rejected."[11] He believed that the Bible was inerrant, "infallibly true,"[12] "the Word of God which remaineth forever."[13] "If there be one false-hood in that book," he wrote, "it did not come from the God of truth."[14]

Some have said that his biblicism was because he lived in a pre-critical age. But this was not the case. Views questioning biblical integrity were beginning to circulate in Europe in the latter part of the eighteenth century. Wesley

simply had no use for them. He gave no credance to
scholars who stood in judgment upon the oracles of God.

Out of this confidence came his commitment to the
doctrines of historic evangelical Christianity. Though he
did not draw up a lengthy creedal statement, like the more
traditional churches, he did take from his Anglican heritage
a simple confession of faith in his "Articles of Religion."
These, with his forty-four standard sermons and *Explanatory Notes Upon the New Testament*, constituted the Methodist "standards" of doctrine.[15]

To contend, as some have, that Methodism has no
"confessional principle" is a distortion of history.[16] It is an
attempt to justify a prevailing liberal theological climate in
the church by imposing upon Wesley a concept of
"pluralism," citing as support his oft-quoted dictum: "As
to all opinions which do not strike at the root of
Christianity, we think and let think."[17]

What is ignored is that Wesley's conciliar principle
applied only to peripheral matters—like modes of baptism
or ecclesiastical forms of government—and was never
intended to excuse deviation from basic biblical revelation.
This deposit of nonnegotiable truth included such foundational doctrines as original sin; the Savior's virgin birth; his
vicarious blood atonement; the bodily resurrection;
Christ's ascension, reign, and triumphant return; and the
judgment to come.

To be sure, the catholic spirit of Wesley cut across all
sectarianism and bigotry. But there could be no toleration
of heresy. Methodist preachers were carefully examined on
the doctrines of the church before being sent to preach.
The model deed to Methodist properties stipulated that the
premises could be used for worship only so long as the
doctrinal standards were faithfully observed.

From this kind of theological stamina flowed Methodist evangelism. It is sheer folly to imagine that the church
today can produce the fruits of the Gospel without similar
doctrinal integrity. There can be no genuine witness nor
growth in spiritual experience, if we do not believe the
Bible message.

GRACE TO ALL

In this bond to the revealed Word of God, Methodist evangelism affirmed the limitless scope of the Gospel invitation, with the consequent mandate to tell the story to every human being.

When it was said that the Son of Man came into the world to save sinners, Wesley understood this to mean that in Christ's redemptive mission there were no exceptions. God loved the world, and to that end finally Jesus died on Calvary. The work was complete. Nothing more needed to be done to provide salvation from all sin for all people.

Here he differed from those of the Reformed tradition, who, in effect, limited the scope of redemption only to the preordained elect. Wesley did not question the absolute sovereignty of God nor the inability of people to save themselves, but he believed that by God's prevenient grace, every person could heed the Gospel call.[18] This was a birthright of the human race. Thus Methodists sang:

> O that the world might taste and see
> The riches of His grace!
> The arms of love that compass me
> Would all mankind embrace.[19]

Driven by this desire, Wesley could not ignore the multitudes yet in darkness. He was especially mindful of those others passed by—the poor, the sick, the illiterate, the outcasts of society—those downtrodden, lonely hearts who felt unwanted and unloved by most churchmen of his day.

When asked how he could justify, on the basis of his catholic spirit, going into other parishes to preach without a proper invitation, Wesley replied:

> Permit me to speak plainly. If by Catholic principles you mean any other than Scriptural, they weigh nothing with me. I allow no other rule, whether of faith or practice, than the Holy Scripture; but on Scriptural principles, I do not think it hard to justify whatever I do. I look upon all the

world as my parish; thus far I mean, that in whatever part of it I am I judge it meet, right, and my bounden duty to declare unto all that are willing to hear, the glad tidings of salvation.[20]

Accordingly, when the bishop of Bristol told Wesley that he had no business in his diocese and ordered him to go hence, the young evangelist refused. For as he explained: "A dispensation of the gospel is committed to me, and woe is me if I preach not the Gospel wherever I am in the habitable world."[21]

That is the burden that still constrains evangelism. Our commission is to go to the lost and to the least—to go to the ends of the earth, crossing every artificial barrier, to take the Gospel to every creature.

Fittingly, the United Methodist hymnal today, just as the first hymn book of Methodism, begins with Charles Wesley's "O for a thousand tongues to sing / My great Redeemer's praise." Then with gaze fixed upon the throne of grace, the prayer is sung:

> My gracious Master and my God,
>   Assist me to proclaim,
> To spread through all the earth abroad
>   The honors of Thy name.[22]

PRAGMATIC METHODOLOGY

Wesley's vision for the masses of humanity was implemented in a relevant methodology. To use contemporary jargon, his methods were contextualized, that is, adapted to the particular culture and needs of the time.

Take Wesley's manner of field preaching as an example. Certainly if he had chosen his own taste in methods, he would never have become an open-air evangelist. Yet he entered upon this new approach because he saw that it was effective in bringing the Gospel to the unchurched multitudes. Later he reflected, "What marvel the devil does not love field preaching! Neither do I; I love a commodious room, a soft cushion, a handsome pulpit.

But where is my zeal, if I do not trample all these underfoot in order to save one more soul?"[23]

Therefore, following the example of Mr. Whitefield, on April 1, 1739, he laid aside his temperamental reservations, and obeyed the controlling mandate to reach the lost. He wrote in his Journal, "At four in the afternoon, I submitted to be more vile, and proclaimed in the highways the glad tidings of salvation, speaking from a little eminence in a ground adjoining to the city, to about 3000 people."[24]

In the next fifty years this was to be his occupation, and field preaching his preeminent style. Wesley took the pace of "an evangelist-at-large."[25] In the out-of-doors in open fields, on street corners, at factory gates, he met the people in congregations larger than church buildings could contain. His biographer Luke Tyerman has computed that of the approximately 500 sermons preached during a nine-month period in 1739, only eight were delivered in churches.[26]

Though often ridiculed and maligned because of his preaching policy, Wesley never quit.[27] What difference did it make that the sophisticated clergymen of his day scorned him? God was using his methods to awaken lost souls to their privileges of grace, and that was all that mattered.

Wesley was so committed to taking the Gospel to the people that he grew impatient when prevented by inclement weather. Indicative of this position, he wrote to one of his young preachers in 1766, "Preach abroad . . . It is the cooping yourselves up in rooms that has damped the work of God, which never was and never will be carried out to any purpose without going out into the highways and hedges and compelling poor sinners to come in."[28]

This compulsion caused Wesley to be utterly pragmatic in planning strategy and establishing policy. Whether his approach was approved by church tradition or his ecclesiastical peers was not of great concern. The question was: Does it work?

Following this rule, he developed the itinerant system of moving preachers from place to place. It seemed at the time, considering resources available, the most expeditious method of ministering to the whole population. By this constraint, also, he started preaching at 5:00 in the morning because he found that it was the best time to catch workers before they went into the mines or factories. The use of lay preachers was justified in the same way, as were extemporaneous prayer, putting Christian hymns to popular tunes, the publishing and distribution of tracts, and, years later, his ordination of ministers.

The organizational structures of class meetings, local societies, and annual conferences were similarly devised. In their particular sphere of government they were simply means of accomplishing the task at hand. Commenting on church practices in a letter to a friend, Wesley asked, "What is the end of all ecclesiastical order? Is it not to bring souls from the power of Satan to God, and to build them up in His fear and love? Order, then, is so far valuable as it answers these ends; and if it answers them not, it is nothing worth."[29]

If we were driven by this criterion today, what effect would it have upon our church policies? Would it not, at the very least, bring us to examine our programs in the light of their fruitfulness? Activities that are seen to be unproductive would be revised, or dropped altogether. And other programs that seem more promising would be tried. The point is that the work must be done, and if what we are presently doing is not working, then we should find out why and do something about it.

For us now in the twentieth century, of course, field preaching or the itinerant system may not be the best recourse. Because these methods were well-suited to Wesley's generation does not necessarily mean that they are conducive to ours. The question is: Are we determined in our situation to get the job done, whatever it takes? When we are, we will discover ways to do it just as those early Methodists did.

DISCIPLINED SAINTHOOD

Woven into this determination to reach sinners was a concern for their growth in the likeness of Christ. Evangelism for Wesley did not end when people made professions of faith. Conversion was only the first step in an ongoing life of discipleship.

Anyone desiring salvation from sins could become a Methodist. But this desire, as Wesley noted, "must be evidenced by three marks: Avoiding all known sin; doing good after his power; and, attending all the ordinances of God."[30] This involved participating in a small class meeting each week, where Methodist discipline was enforced. These informal gatherings were ideally suited to those persons seeking a congenial place to express their personal fears and needs, and for this reason they probably contributed more to the growth of the church than any other program.[31]

The class leader was expected to inquire of each person how his soul prospered, and "to advise, reprove, comfort, or exhort" as the occasion required.[32] In this manner, no Methodist was ever left without regular oversight. Failure to attend these meetings automatically disqualified one for continued membership in the society.

Smaller groups of people met each week in bands. These meetings were for the purpose of recounting Christian experiences and plainly confessing faults. The leader of each band was required to describe "his own state first, and then to ask the rest, in order, as many and as searching questions as may be, concerning their state, sins, and temptations."[33] One can imagine the cathartic effect this regular exercise had upon the people.

Conditions for admission to the societies, summed up in the *General Rules*, required of every Methodist adherence to a high degree of piety, at least, in outward manifestations. This acceptable conduct involved both detachment from common personal vices like "buying or selling spiritous liquors" and working on the Sabbath; and positive acts of concern for the physical and spiritual needs of humanity. Moreover, as the rules stated:

> If there be any among us who observe them not, who habitually break any of them, let it be made known unto them who watch over that soul as they that must give an account. We will admonish him of the error of his ways; we will bear with him for a season; but then if he repent not, he hath no more place among us. We have delivered our souls.[34]

Methodists were expected to live holy lives. Perfection of love was always held before them as the standard—a love that found expression toward God in purity of devotion and toward people in selfless service. Out of such holiness flowed their personal witness and social compassion.

Herein was the attraction of their evangelism. It was beautiful in practical holiness. No wonder Wesley exhorted his preachers to follow his example in continually speaking on Christian perfection. "Speak and spare not," he said. "Let not regard for man induce you to betray the truth of God. Till you press the believers to expect full salvation now you must not look for any revival."[35]

It is still true today. Evangelism without holiness, both in the witness and the fruit desired, becomes a contradiction. We must recover not only the Wesleyan standard of Christian character, but also the disciplined manner by which that life is encouraged. Merely recruiting church members is not enough; new converts must be nourished in a lifestyle of holiness—a Christlikeness that inevitably radiates love to a lost world.

BODY MINISTRY

Out of such commitment the whole church was mobilized for ministry. Wesley's holistic approach did more than meet the felt needs of people; he involved them in the ongoing work. Early Methodism took seriously the priesthood of all believers. This was immediately evident in the atmosphere created within the class and band meetings. In these little groups of kindred spirits, everyone was enabled to participate in the ministry of counseling, encouragement, and prayer. What a natural way to stimulate mutual expression of love, an emphasis inherent in their holiness ethic! From the very beginning of incorporation in the body, they were learning to function as priests by ministering to each other.

Within this context, persons with special gifts would be recognized, and some, appropriately endowed, made class and band leaders. Those with different gifts might be appointed stewards or assigned some other form of service. Significantly, the pastoral functions of ministry, including visiting the sick, comforting the bereaved, and looking after the destitute, were carried on largely by the local people themselves.

Even the preachers appointed by Wesley to the circuits were usually laymen, without any professional training for ministry. In fact, for the most part they had little or no formal education. They were people who came up from the ranks—God-fearing men and women who sensed the call of God for this kind of service.

The use of lay preachers provoked criticism by the more educated clergy of other communions, of course. Augustus Toplady, for example, accused Wesley of "prostituting the ministerial function to the lowest and most illiterate mechanics, persons of almost any class." Further reflecting his disdain, as well as the extent of Methodist lay involvement, Toplady advised, "Let his cobblers keep to their stalls. Let his tinkers mind their vessels. Let his barbers confine themselves to their blocks and basons. Let his bakers stand to their kneading troughs. Let his blacksmiths blow more suitable coals than those of controversy."[36]

Yet this is our Methodist heritage. We have come from the workshops of common laborers, not theological seminaries. Wesley did not belittle ordination, nor university training. He was himself a college man, probably one of the most thoroughly educated clergymen of his day. But he knew that any evangelistic movement that reaches the masses must bring its own people into harvest.

We, too, must learn to multiply ourselves by equipping others for the work of ministry. I am afraid that most descendants of Wesley today have little personal sense of responsibility for reaching the world. The theory of every-member involvement is there, but by our example, one would get the impression that ministry requires professional training and ecclesiastical sanction. It is imperative that the daily work of making disciples through our vocational callings be rediscovered. Whatever our gifts, there is a ministry for all, not only in testifying to the grace of God but in helping new Christians assume their role in the Great Commission.

THE SPIRIT OF PENTECOST

Fusing all of this together in a mighty movement of evangelism was the power of the Spirit of God. This reality, on a personal level, gave direction to the experience of salvation, and preserved Wesley's biblical theology from the complacency of dead orthodoxy. It was the refining fire of Pentecost that inflamed them with love for a lost world, and constrained them, by any means at hand, to herald the Gospel to every creature. By the same mighty in-working of the energizing Spirit, they were brought under godly discipline, and molded into an army of laborers.

Here was the genius of Methodism. It was not another religious institution, but a movement of renewal, joining together earnest souls seeking first the kingdom. To the question in the *Larger Minutes*, "What may we measurably believe to be God's design in raising up the preachers called Methodists?" Wesley answered, "Not to form any new sect; but to reform the nation, particularly the church; and to spread Scriptural holiness over the land."[37]

In keeping with this objective, Methodists were advised to attend their parish churches, and there to be a savoring influence for "genuine Christianity."[38] Hence, one could be a Methodist without leaving one's own communion or even becoming a member of a Methodist society. Their purpose was to "spread life among all denominations," wrote Wesley in 1790, though he added prophetically, "Which they will do til they form a separate sect."[39]

For more than forty years Methodism existed as an ecumenical body in the midst of and alongside established churches. Accused of being "a church within a church," Wesley responded by saying: "That church, if she knew her own interest, would see she is much obliged to us for so doing."[40] Certainly the parachurch nature of the original societies was seen as no impediment to their spiritual effectiveness. Indeed, "it could be argued," according to A. Skevington Wood, a foremost Methodist historian, that "Wesley's societies were most useful when they remained independent of ecclesiastical control, whether Anglican or eventually Methodist."[41]

Ponder the implications of this for our day. If the power of Methodism is somehow diminished when institutionalized, why should we feel so obliged to perpetuate the ecclesiastical structures? Would we not more nearly represent the vision of Wesley by concentrating our energy upon developing spiritual resources rather than bureaucratic organizations?

By the same criterion, why should we limit our fellowship to those within the Methodist constituency? In the true Wesleyan catholic spirit, do we not have affinity with people from every denominational background who are in the flow of revival, be they Baptist, Lutheran, Pentecostal, or something else? Indeed, are not our ties in the Spirit much closer to these persons of kindred hearts and aspirations than any loyalty to a particular denomination? Then let us cultivate our oneness with the movement of God's Spirit in our time.

NEVER-DYING PRAISE

Last summer my wife and I had opportunity to visit John Wesley's house in London. It was especially moving to enter the little room in which he breathed his last. One who was present when he died has written that as Wesley's strength failed, with great exertion, he cried: "The best of all is, God is with us!" And then, as if to comfort his weeping friends kneeling by the bedside, "lifting up his dying arm in token of victory, and raising his feeble voice with a holy triumph not to be expressed, he again repeated the heart-reviving words, 'The best of all is, God is with us!' "[42] Thereafter, in the few remaining hours that his soul lingered between earth and heaven, he was heard again and again to whisper, "I'll praise . . . I'll praise! . . ."[43]

Picturing that scene in my mind, I asked the custodian of the house whether my wife and I could be alone in the room for a few minutes and he obliged. What a precious time it was! We knelt together by the bed, and as our spirits joined his praise of the Most High, with the church victorious of every name and tongue and nation, we gave thanks for what God has wrought through the witness of that man with a burning heart. And best of all, God is still with us.

NOTES

[1] Adapted from a description of this event by Halford E. Luccock and Paul Hutchinson, *The Story of Methodism* (New York: Abingdon-Cokesbury, 1926), 13–18.

[2] Wesley, *Journal* 1:475–76. The description of this experience as well as the struggles leading up to it indicate that it was for Wesley an evangelical conversion. Though there were evidences of spiritual awakening much earlier, as far back as 1725, it was not until Aldersgate that a complete turning point in his life became obvious. Commentary on this position may be found in J. E. Rattenbury, *The Conversion of the Wesleys* (London: Epworth, 1938).

[3] Wesley, *Journal* 1:476.

[4] This hymn of Charles Wesley is generally believed to be the one sung on this occasion, though it is not named by either John or Charles. Another possibility, sometimes proposed, is Wesley's "And Can It Be," of which the last two stanzas appropriately voice a confident testimony. See Thomas Jackson, *The Life of the Rev. Charles Wesley*, vol. 1 (London: John Mason, 1841), 137–38; and D. M. Jones, *Charles Wesley, A Study* (London: Skeffington & Son, n.d.), 71–73.

⁵John Wesley, "The Witness of the Spirit," Discourse II, *The Works of John Wesley,* ed. Thomas Jackson, 14 vols. (Grand Rapids: Zondervan), 5:125.

⁶John Wesley, *A Short History of Methodism, Works,* Jackson ed., 8:348. In his *A Plain Account of Christian Perfection,* Ibid., 9:367, he mentions the year 1729 as the time when the Bible became for him "the only standard of truth."

⁷Wesley, *Letters,* 2:244.

⁸Wesley, *Works,* 8:349; cf. *Works,* 7:198.

⁹Wesley, *Journal,* 5:169.

¹⁰Examples are Wesley's comments on John 19:24; 1 Corinthians 2:13; and Galatians 3:8 in his *Explanatory Notes Upon the New Testament* (New York: Lane & Tippett, 1847), 268, 412, 478.

¹¹Wesley, Ibid., note on John 10:35, p. 245.

¹²John Wesley, "The Means of Grace," *Wesley's Standard Sermons,* ed. Edward H. Sugden, 2 vols. (London: Epworth, 1968), 1:249–50.

¹³Wesley, *Explanatory Notes,* Preface, par. 10.

¹⁴Wesley, *Journal,* 6:117. In this same notation on August 24, 1776, he refutes the notion of a Soame Jenyn that the writers of the Bible could have made some mistakes. For an excellent summary of Wesley's regard for Scripture, see A. Skevington Wood, *The Burning Heart— John Wesley: Evangelist* (Minneapolis: Bethany Fellowship, 1978), 209–19.

¹⁵When the Constitution of the Methodist Episcopal Church was established at the General Conference of 1808, the First Restrictive Rule of the Constitution "prohibited any change, alteration, or addition" to these standards, *Discipline* (1988), 54. For a competent summary of the historic Methodist standards of doctrine, see Thomas C. Oden, *Doctrinal Standards in the Wesleyan Tradition* (Grand Rapids: Zondervan/Francis Asbury Press, 1988). The changes that have come in Methodist theology from Wesley's day to the middle twentieth century are reviewed by Robert E. Chiles, *Theological Transition in American Methodism: 1790–1935* (New York: Abingdon, 1965).

¹⁶This was the position taken by the General Conference of 1972, as noted in *The Book of Discipline of the United Methodist Church, 1980* (Nashville: United Methodist Publishing House, 1980), 41. The General Conference of 1988 tempered this view by affirming "the primacy of Scripture" in the formation of doctrinal standards. It would appear that tradition, experience, and reason, components of the Methodist quadrilateral, are now understood officially as being subordinate to Scripture. Ibid., 41, 81–86.

¹⁷*Discipline* (1980), 40.

¹⁸In this conviction, Methodism followed in the Arminian theological tradition, though it was more aggressively evangelistic in spirit and practical in its application. Wilbur F. Tillett expressed it well

when he said, "The theology of Wesley and his followers is the Arminianism of Holland baptized with the Holy Ghost and infused with spiritual life," quoted by Thomas Benjamin Neely, *Doctrinal Standards of Methodism* (New York: Revell, 1918), 127–28.

[19]Charles Wesley, from the hymn "Jesus, the Name High Over All."

[20]Wesley, *Letters* 1:285–86.

[21]Wesley, *Journal* 2:257.

[22]Charles Wesley, from the hymn "O for a Thousand Tongues to Sing."

[23]Wesley, *Journal*, 4:325.

[24]Ibid., 2:156.

[25]Skevington Wood, 98.

[26]Luke Tyerman, *The Life and Times of the Rev. John Wesley*, 3 vols. (New York: Harper, 1870–71), 1:234.

[27]Examples are cited by Skevington Wood, 94–97.

[28]Wesley, *Letters*, 5:13.

[29]Ibid., 2:77.

[30]Wesley, "On God's Vineyard," *Works*, 7:209. Actually this is but a summation of the requirements for continuing in a Methodist society specified in the "General Rules," *Discipline* (1988), 75–77.

[31]From the standpoint of evangelistic strategy, since the class meeting was so central to early Methodist growth, it would be well to become acquainted with this program. For a basic introduction to the activity, read John Wesley's "Rules of the Band Societies," *Works*, 8:272–73. For some commentary on the practice, see "The Difficulties and Trials Connected with the Office of a Leader," by Charles C. Keep, in Frederick A. Norwood, ed., *Sourcebook of American Methodism*, (Nashville: Abingdon, 1982), 162–66. Among the many contemporary authors who have written on the class meeting are Howard Snyder, David Lowes Watson, Samuel Emerick, Gloster S. Udy, and Allan Coppedge.

[32]Wesley, *A Plain Account of the People Called Methodist, Works* 8:253.

[33]Wesley, *Rules of the Band Societies, Works*, Ibid., 272.

[34]*The Nature, Design, and General Rules of the United Societies*, drawn up by Wesley in 1743, and thereafter included in all editions of the United Methodist *Discipline*. (See p. 77 of the 1988 edition.)

[35]Wesley, *Letters*, 4:321.

[36]Quoted by Howard A. Snyder, *The Radical Wesley* (Downers Grove: InterVarsity Press, 1980), 64.

[37]Wesley, *Minutes of Several Conversations, Works*, 8:299.

[38]Wesley, "Remarks on a Defence of Aspasio Vindicated," *Works*, 10:351.

[39]Wesley, *Letters*, 8:211.

[40]Wesley, "Defense of Aspasio," *Works*, 10:352.

[41] Skevington Wood, 193.

[42] Account written by Betsy Ritchie, "Wesley's Last Hours," in *The Heart of John Wesley's Journal*, ed. Percy Livingston Parker (New Canaan, Conn.: Keats, 1979), xxix.

[43] Ibid.

CHAPTER TWO:

The Lostness of Mankind

FLEEING FROM THE WRATH TO COME

In 1760 a group of Protestants from Ireland migrated to New York. Among them were some Methodists, including Philip Embury, a young carpenter, who had been a local preacher in the old country. In the company, too, was a married woman, a cousin of Embury, named Barbara Heck.

As is still often true of people who are uprooted, the newcomers settled down to a life of church inactivity, a state certainly different from their Methodist heritage. Things drifted on for five years without any organized worship. It was Mrs. Heck who finally took the initiative. One day coming across a group of men gambling in a card game, the aroused woman grabbed the cards, threw them into the fire, and proceeded to exhort the men to repent. Then, while still distressed, she rushed to the house of Embury, and cried, "You must preach to us or we shall all go to hell, and God will require our blood at your hands."[1]

It was not long before a little group of anxious souls gathered in Embury's house, and the Methodist movement was underway in America. Just as their predecessors across the ocean, the "decision to flee from the wrath to come and to be saved from their sins" brought them together.[2] Indeed, as stated in the *General Rules*, this was the only condition required of those seeking admission into a society. More hopeful truth of Christian doctrine must be perceived, of course, but the sense of impending doom awaiting sinners made the option of salvation good news indeed.

PREACHING ON JUDGMENT

That persons hearing Methodist preachers would be brought to this conclusion can be seen in a not uncommon sermon of John Wesley on "The Way to the Kingdom."[3] Using as his text Mark 1:15, "The Kingdom of God is at hand: Repent ye, and believe the Gospel," he went on to describe the nature of true religion as "righteousness, and peace, and joy in the Holy Ghost," emphasizing that this kingdom can be entered now.

With this blessing of God in focus, he turned to the human responsibility to repent, graphically describing the corruption of the sinner's heart:

> And knowest thou not that "the wages of sin is death"?—death, not only temporal, but eternal. "The soul that sinneth, it shall die"; for the mouth of the Lord hath spoken it . . . This is the sentence, to "be punished" with never-ending death, "with everlasting destruction from the presence of the Lord, and from the glory of his power." Knowest thou not that every sinner . . . "is in danger of hell-fire"; that expression is far too weak; but rather, "is under the sentence of hell-fire"; doomed already, just dragging to execution. Thou art guilty of everlasting death. It is the just reward of thy inward and outward wickedness. It is just that the sentence should now take place. Dost thou see, dost thou feel this? Art thou thoroughly convinced that thou deservest God's wrath, and everlasting damnation? Would God do thee no wrong, if he now commanded the earth to open,

and swallow thee up? if thou went now to go down quick into the pit, into the fire that never shall be quenched? If God hath given thee truely to repent, thou hast a deep sense that these things are so; and that it is of his mere mercy thou art not consumed, swept away from the face of the earth.

At this point Wesley raises the question, "And what wilt thou do to appease the wrath of God, to atone for all thy sins, and to escape the punishment thou hast so justly deserved?" The answer is obvious. "Alas, thou canst do nothing; nothing that will in anywise make amends to God for one evil work, or word, or thought." But in the realization of total helplessness, he added, if there be "sorrow of heart . . . and the earnest desire to cease from evil," then "thou art not far from the kingdom . . . Thou dost 'repent.'"

He then lifts up Christ's atoning work "to save sinners," and quotes John 3:16. "Believe this," he says, "and the kingdom of God is thine." After explaining what faith means, Wesley stresses again the love of God, and the joy that awaits all those who receive his grace. "Now cast thyself on the Lamb of God, with all thy sins," he pleads, "and 'an entrance shall' now 'be ministered unto thee, into the kingdom of our Lord and Saviour Jesus Christ!'"

Such was Methodist preaching. They believed that lost men and women not only must be warned of their danger, but also called to decision. Their writings are filled with references to sermons preached from such texts as: "The time is short"; "Turn from darkness to light, and from the power of Satan unto God"; "Prepare to meet thy God"; "Say unto them . . . I have no pleasure in the death of the wicked."[4] The comment of Francis Asbury after delivering a message on 2 Corinthians 5:11, "Knowing the terror of the Lord, we persuade men," might well express the attitude of all the itinerants. He wrote, "If the people say it was like thunder and lightning[,] I shall not be surprised. I spoke in power from God, and there was a general and deep feeling in the congregation: thine, O Lord, be all the glory!"[5]

A PASSING CONVICTION

Nothing quite so contradicts evangelism as indifference to the lostness of mankind. An atheist expressed it well when he wrote:

> Did I firmly believe, as millions say they do, that the knowledge and practice of religion in this life influences destiny in another . . . I would esteem one soul gained for heaven worth a life of suffering. Earthly consequences should never stay my hand, nor seal my lips . . . I would strive to look upon eternity alone and on the immortal souls around me, soon to be everlasting happy or everlasting miserable. I would go forth to the world and preach it in season and out of season, and my text would be "What shall it profit a man if he gain the world and lose his soul."[6]

The question should provoke an answer. I am afraid, however, that a United Methodist bishop, reflecting upon the decline of evangelistic passion in the church, was perceptive when he commented to a gathering of ministers, "Our trouble is that we don't believe anymore that people are lost."

Judging from the actions of average Methodists, as well as from official pronouncements of the church, the bishop's impression may not be far off the mark.[7] It is not that the biblical teachings respecting God's judgment are openly denied, but that this area of truth is ignored.[8]

The same pertains to the state of persons caught within the web of non-Christian religions. By listening to the rhetoric of our leaders and from reading the literature churned out by our church agencies, one would be hard pressed to validate the exclusive claims of the Gospel, that whoever does not come to Christ stands condemned "because he has not believed in the name of God's one and only Son" (John 3:18, NIV).[9]

In fairness it should be said, however, that this indifference is not peculiar to the people called Methodist. Martin Marty, eminent church historian at the University of Chicago, has keenly observed that "the passing of hell from modern consciousness is one of the major, if still undocumented major trends," of our time.[10] After all, a generation preoccupied with immediate sensual gratification is not likely to think much about the eternal consequences of sin.

THE NEW THINKING

The popular sentiment, whether consciously espoused or not, is the notion that finally all people will be saved. Proponents of this universalism believe that God is too good to send anyone to hell, or conversely, that folk are too good to be damned. In either case, the teachings of Christ regarding retribution for sin are naïvely circumvented, while the atoning purpose of his cross is effectively denied. Jesus' death becomes little more than the martyrdom of a great moral teacher.

Neo-orthodox divines, like Karl Barth, may have a higher appreciation of our Lord's sacrifice, but they come to the same conclusion. Their contention is that God's power is so great that nothing can prevail against His love, even if it requires a period of purgation and another opportunity for salvation after death.

One has to ask, however, if all will be saved regardless of their rebellion against God, why call sinners to repentance? Does not preaching the Gospel become superfluous? If evangelism is nothing more than trying to improve living conditions in this world, what hope is there for the dying?

TEACHING OF CHRIST

The issue comes back to the authority of Scripture. Devastating as it may be to human pride, the Bible records Jesus saying that when the Son of Man shall return to judge the living and the dead, "he will separate the people one from another as a shepherd separates the sheep from the goats . . . Then he will say to those on his left, 'Depart from me, you who are cursed, into the eternal fire prepared for the devil and his angels' . . . Then they will go away to eternal punishment" (Matt. 25:31–46, NIV).[11]

Clearly our Lord taught that those who turn to their own way shall be sentenced to a place of conscious separation from God and the loss of all that is good, including heaven. It is this "banishment from the presence of the Lord," Wesley says, that is "the very essence of destruction." What makes the loss so terrifying to the soul is the knowledge then "that God alone is the center of all created spirits, and, in consequence, that a spirit made for God can have no rest out of Him."[12]

This is called the "hell of fire" (e.g., Matt. 18:9; cf. Matt. 13:41–42; 25:41–46; Mark 9:43–44; John 5:28–29; Luke 12:5);[13] a habitation of "outer darkness; in that place there shall be weeping and gnashing of teeth" (Matt. 8:12); a night where the cries of the damned never die and "the fire is not quenched" (Mark 9:48).[14] These and many other words of Christ, though in part figurative, unequivocally warn us of the awful fact of hell. Furthermore, He said that most people are following a "broad way," which leads to this "destruction" (Matt. 7:13).

FACING REALITY

Jesus is not trying to scare anyone. He simply wants us to face the fact that human existence does not end at the grave, and that unless the course of one's life is reversed, the penal consequences of sin continue on forever. It is unending death, a state in which the immortal soul can never die to its misery, never know relief.[15] "Fear not them which kill the body, and are not able to kill the soul," Jesus said, "but rather fear him which is able to destroy both soul and body in hell" (Matt. 10:28, KJV).

The question is, do we believe the Word? In his letter to William Law, John Wesley put it very pointedly:

> Now this much cannot be denied, that these texts speak as if there were really such a place as hell . . .

I would then ask but one plain question: If the case is not so, why did God speak as if it was? Say you, "To affright men from sin"? What, by guile, by dissimulation, by hanging out false colours? Can you conceive the Most High dressing up a scarecrow, as we do to fright children? Far be it from Him! If there be any such fraud in the Bible, the Bible is not of God. And indeed this must be the result of all: If there be "no unquenchable fire, no everlasting burnings," there is no dependence on these writings wherein they are so expressly asserted, nor of the eternity of heaven, any more than of hell. So that if we give up the one, we must give up the other. No hell, no heaven, no revelation![16]

THE LOVE OF GOD

Admittedly, the prospect of everlasting torment is not a pleasant thought. Most of us would like to believe that God is too loving to consign a person to unremitting remorse. What we may fail to realize is that God cannot violate His own integrity. Though infinite in love, He is also holy—of purer eyes than to behold evil—and He cannot ignore the sin that would destroy His beloved. "It is not because God's love is limited," as Donald Bloesch notes, "but because it is unlimited" that hell as well as heaven is made necessary.[17] The wrath of God is only the other side of His love, a love that will never let us go, even when decreeing justice.

Yes, love like this is painful, and no one has suffered more in contemplating its cost than our Lord. Calvary is His witness. Seeing our utter lostness, God took upon Himself in the Person of His Son the judgment due us all. Such love is too wonderful for us to fathom, but we can bear witness to its ever-present reality, that "while we were yet sinners, Christ died for us" (Rom. 5:8).

This is the Gospel that must be proclaimed, the amazing truth that the Creator and Lord of the universe has intervened in human history, and through the mighty conquest of His Son, made a way whereby "whosoever believes in Him shall not perish, but have everlasting life" (John 3:16). But in heralding this good news, its corallary must also be told, that "he who does not obey the Son shall not see life, but the wrath of God abides on him" (John 3:36; cf. 3:18; 1 John 5:12). Hell is reserved for those who scorn God's love by trampling under their feet the blood of Christ.

THOSE WHO HAVE NOT HEARD

But what about those multitudes who have never heard an intelligent presentation of the Way of Life, two-thirds of the world's population living in darkness, usually in the bondage of false religion or idolatrous materialism? More tragically, at the present time, most of these unreached people have no one of their culture and language near enough to them to make clear what the Gospel means. Does their ignorance excuse them from the judgment of hell?[18]

Those who reject the basic tenets of Scripture, of course, are not bothered with this, for they can dismiss the teachings of Christ that He alone is "the way and the truth and the life" (John 14:6; cf. Acts 4:12). To them all roads lead to God, and while Christianity may have superior insights, still they believe that all religions have redeeming worth to their devotees. What matters to them is not God's revelation in His Son, but sincerity of conviction, whatever it might be. It might be allowed, for example, that whether one follows Christ or Buddha is inconsequential so long as the person lives up to his or her faith.

The problem with this view is that sincerity does not change error. A man may mistakingly board a plane for New York thinking that he is going to Los Angeles, but that does not change his destination. When sincerity becomes the criterion for salvation, there is no way a confused, self-centered people can determine right from wrong, and finally they become a law unto themselves (Rom. 2:14–15).

Nor does it help things by saying that persons who do

not believe in Christ can follow the light they have in general revelation. For who has ever perfectly responded to all the opportunities to know God through the natural world? This is why everyone is "without excuse" and given over "to a depraved mind" (Rom. 1:18–32). The Scripture has concluded that all have sinned and come short of the glory of our Creator (Rom. 3:23).

Let it be understood, though, that God is found by those who truly seek Him, and to those who walk in the light that they have, He is pleased to give more light (Mark 4:25; Matt. 7:7; 13:12).[19] We can affirm that by the prevenience of God's grace everyone has been given sufficient light to come to the truth. So responsibility for salvation rests finally with each individual.

IS THERE ANOTHER WAY?

Does this mean that one can be saved without a knowledge of God's redeeming work in Christ? To this, I can answer only that if such an alternative exists, it has not been disclosed to us. Therefore, for me to offer hope of salvation through any other name would be morally wrong. God, within His own nature, can do whatever He pleases. But I can act only on the basis of His Word.

An analogy of Dr. Robertson McQuilkin may be helpful at this point.[20] He compares a Christian to a security guard charged with the protection of residents on the tenth floor of a nursing home. Among other things, it is his responsibility to get the patients to safety should an emergency arise. Accordingly, he is given a floor plan to the building, which delineates clearly where the fire exits are located. Should a fire break out, what would you feel toward the guard if, rather than following instructions, he discussed with the residents the possibility of there being other escape routes than those indicated on the map? Or suppose that he suggested that it may not be necessary to go down the steps at all, for he had heard a report of someone who had jumped from a ten-story building and survived? Would you not think the man terribly foolish, if not criminally negligent?

Yet I am afraid that that is how many of us have acted toward the command of our Lord to take the Gospel to every creature. Oh, yes, in our minds we still declare our loyalty to the creeds; but by our casual attitude to the lost multitudes, one may wonder how deeply the meaning of the Cross has penetrated our hearts.

A BURDEN TO RECOVER

Would that we could recover the burden for a perishing world felt so deeply by our Methodist progenitors! Not that we would become morbid in its contemplation, least of all insensitive to the feelings of persons who do not believe.[21] No one can think of hell and be judgmental, for we know that except for the grace of God we would be as those without hope.

Yet the sense of our Lord's overwhelming grace and all its attendant joy cannot wash away the tears that flow at the thought of multitudes unsaved. Realizing their impending doom, we must reach out to them with the Word of Life, "warning every man and teaching every man in all wisdom" (Col. 1:28, KJV).

Reflecting upon this admonition of the apostle Paul, Bishop Francis Asbury, not long before he died, expressed his apprehension that many who had been taught the Gospel were now "negligent" in sounding its warning. Then, as if exhorting himself, he wrote in his Journal:

> Tell this rebellious generation they are already condemned, and will be shortly damned; preach to them like Moses from Mount Sinai and Ebal, like David—"The wicked shall be turned into hell, and all the nations that forget God"; like Isaiah— "Who amongst you shall dwell with everlasting burnings?"; like Ezekiel—"O, wicked men! thou shall surely die!" Pronounce the eight woes uttered by the Son of God near the close of his ministry, and ask with him—"Ye serpents, ye generation of

vipers, how can ye escape the damnation of hell?"
Preach as if you had seen heaven and its celestial
inhabitants and had hovered over the bottomless
pit and beheld the tortures and heard the groans of
the damned.[22]

When have you last heard preaching like this? It may
run counter to the prevailing universalism of our culture,
but it is our Wesleyan heritage. And if we want to see the
fruits of evangelism in our day as did the early disciples of
Wesley, we would do well to emulate their example. One
thing is sure: if we believe there is a hell, we cannot ignore
the lost nor withhold the good news that Jesus saves all who
will come to God through Him.

A SOMBER WARNING

Let us be aware, too, that some day we ourselves must
give account for our stewardship of the Gospel, for "we
shall all stand before the judgment seat of Christ" (Rom.
14:10, KJV). Preaching on this text in 1758, before one of
the judges of His Majesty's Court of Common Pleas in St.
Paul's Church at Bedford, John Wesley closed his message
with this plea:

O, who can stand before the face of the great God,
even our Saviour Jesus Christ!

See! See! He cometh! He maketh the clouds His
chariots! He rideth upon the wings of the wind!

A devouring fire goeth before Him, and after Him
a flame burneth! See! He sitteth upon His throne,
clothed with light as with a garment, arrayed with
majesty and honour! Behold, His eyes are as a
flame of fire, His voice as the sound of many
waters!

. . . Hear the Lord, the Judge! "Come, ye blessed
of my Father, inherit the kingdom prepared for
you from the foundation of the world." Joyful
sound! How widely different than that voice which
echoes through the expanse of heaven, "Depart, ye

cursed, into everlasting fire, prepared for the devil and his angels!" And who is he that can prevent or retard the full execution of either sentence? . . .

"What manner of persons then ought we to be, in all holy conversation and godliness?" We know it cannot be long before the Lord will descend with the voice of the archangel, and the trumpet of God; when everyone of us shall appear before Him, and give account of his own works. "Wherefore, beloved, seeing ye look for these things," seeing ye know He will come and will not tarry, "be diligent, that ye may be found of Him in peace," without spot and blameless. Why should ye not? Why should one of you be found on the left hand at His appearing? He willeth not that any should perish, but that all should come to repentance; by repentance, to faith in a bleeding Lord; by faith, to spotless love, to the full image of God renewed in the heart, and producing all holiness of conversation. Can you doubt of this, when you remember the Judge of all is likewise the Savior of all? Hath He not bought you with His own blood, that ye might not perish, but have everlasting life? O make proof of His mercy, rather than His justice; of His love, rather than the thunder of His power![23]

NOTES

[1] Luccock, *The Story of Methodism*, 147.
[2] "General Rules," *Discipline* (1988), 48, 74–77.
[3] Wesley, *Works*, 5:76–86.
[4] Examples can be seen in Jesse Lee, *Journal*, in *Memoir of the Rev. Jesse Lee with Extracts from His Journals*, by Minton Thrift (New York: N. Bangs and T. Mason, 1823), 65, 126, 357; Asbury, *Journal and Letters*, 2:786, 788, 796; Peter Cartwright, *Autobiography of Peter Cartwright, the Backwoods Preacher*, ed. W. P. Strickland (New York: Methodist Book Concern, 1856), 145.
[5] Asbury, *Journal and Letters*, 2:745, cf. 788.
[6] Quoted in Norman Grubb, *C. T. Studd* (Atlantic City: World Wide Prayer Movement, 1935), 40.
[7] "Our Doctrinal Heritage" adopted at the 1988 General Conference is a good illustration. Contrary to the older "doctrinal standards,"

the new document says nothing about the judgment of God nor the separation of the wicked in hell, *Discipline* (1988), 40–50. It may be argued that there was no need to reaffirm truths already accepted by the church since the older Articles of Religion of the Methodist Episcopal Church speak of Christ returning "to judge all men at the last day" (Article III), and the Confession of Faith of the Evangelical United Brethren, in allusion to this judgment, speaks of the wicked being assigned to "endless condemnation" (Articles II, XII). However, if the contemporary restatement of "Our Doctrinal Heritage" is truly historical and reflective of the original faith of the church, why were these doctrines omitted? The most reasonable conclusion is that the theologians who drew up the position purposefully sought to make present-day Methodist teaching more compatible with the prevailing humanism of our society. In this respect, the present statement represents the same weak, pluralistic thought of the 1972 General Conference.

[8] Not even in describing "Our Theological Task" is there any cognizance of the need to warn the ungodly of divine wrath, *Discipline* (1988), 77–90. As we would expect, there is appropriate recognition of the challenges to theology generated by great human struggles for liberation and personal fulfillment, but the satanic power of evil captivating the souls of men and women is utterly overlooked. Likewise, the "Social Principles" of the church, predictably concerned about such problems as exploitation, the ecological causes, population, nuclear weapons, transnational business organizations, and the like, fail to mention the ultimate problem of a dying race, *Discipline* (1988), 91–111. Incredible as it may seem, while giving lip service to the "doctrinal standards" of the church, the General Conferences for generations, by omission and innuendo, have undermined evangelism.

[9] An example of this evasion is the missional section on "The Ministry of All Christians" in the *Discipline* (1988), 112–19. Nowhere does the document make clear that believing in Jesus Christ makes any difference whether a person is saved or lost. Merely repeating words about "outgoing love" and "servanthood" does not answer the question of universalism in world missions.

[10] *Evangelical Beacon* 59, no. 13 (June 23, 1986), 15.

[11] Commenting on the reference to the "fire prepared for the devil and his angels," Wesley mused, "And who can doubt but that their infernal spirits will immediately execute the sentence; will instantly drag those forsaken by God into their own place of torment," in his sermon "The Important Question," *Works*, 6:497.

[12] John Wesley, "Of Hell," *Works* 6:383, 385. Elaborating on this "punishment of loss," he says, "There is no grandeur in the infernal regions; there is nothing beautiful in those dark abodes; no light but that of livid flames. And nothing new, but one unvaried scene of horror . . . Nor is there anything to gratify the sense of honour. No; they are the heirs of shame and everlasting contempt." He goes on to say that to this

anguish is added "The punishment of sense," which implies "unspeakable misery . . . a guilty conscience . . . self-condemnation . . . unholy
tempers; envy, malice, revenge, all of which incessantly grieve the soul."
Compare a similar statement in "An Extract on a Letter to the Reverend
Mr. Law," *Works*, 9:506. Developing this idea of estrangement,
speaking on "Human Life a Dream," Wesley depicts hell as a prison,
whose inhabitants are seen as "emblems of the rage against God and man
. . . causing them to gnash their teeth at Him they so long despised,"
Works, 7:323.

13 This term is recorded eleven times on the lips of Jesus, and
always refers to a place of destruction. A different term, "hades," refers
to the place of departed spirits, or as Wesley notes, "literally the
invisible world, whether good or bad." From his sermon on "Dives and
Lazarus," *Works*, Ibid., 247; cf. the same observation in "Our Faith,"
Ibid., 327; and "The Discovery of Faith," Ibid., 234.

14 The horror of this fire, Wesley says, is that the soul is not
consumed. "There is no end! What a thought!" He ponders, "Every
suffering is softened, if there is any hope, though distant, of deliverance
from it. But here, hope never comes . . . When they are cast unto the
fire . . . their worm dieth not, and the fire is not quenched." "Of Hell,"
Works, 6:390.

15 In his sermon "On Eternity," Wesley contemplates this endless
state: "Why, if we were only to be chained down one day, yea, one hour,
in a lake of fire, how amazingly long would one day or one hour appear. I
know not if it would not seem as a thousand years. But (astonishing
thought) after thousand or thousands, he has just tasted of his bitter cup!
After millions, it will be no nearer the end than it was the moment it
began," Ibid., 194.

16 A letter of John Wesley to Mr. Law, dated January 6, 1756, in
Letters 3:370; see the whole letter, which deals with the issue of the fall
of mankind and its consequences, 332–70.

17 Donald G. Bloesch, *Essentials of Evangelical Theology*, 2 vols.
(New York: Harper, 1979), 2:224–25.

18 On this question, John Wesley wisely observed that "we are not
required to determine anything touching their final state. How it will
please God, the Judge of all, to deal with them, we may leave to God
himself." Wesley's sermon "On Charity," *Works*, 8:47.

19 Wesley's comment is that God is "rich in mercy to all that call
upon him, according to the light they have." Ibid., 7:47f.

20 Robertson McQuilkin, *The Great Omission* (Grand Rapids:
Baker, 1984), 51.

21 It may be well to note that the *Minutes* drawn up by Wesley in
1745 raised the question: "Do not some of our assistants preach too
much of the wrath, and too little of the love of God?" To which he
answered: "We fear they have leaned to that extreme; and hence some of
their hearers may have lost the joy of faith." It appears that this issue

was raised because some Methodists were preaching "hell, fire and damnation" too much in the regular services. Wesley goes on to explain that the love of God is a much stronger motive for response. *Works,* 8:284. The following year, in a letter to John Smith, Wesley cautioned against "the profuse throwing about of hell and damnation." *Letters,* 2:69.

22 A notation of Francis Asbury under the Sabbath, July 9, 1815, *Journal and Letters,* 2:784–85. Asbury died less than a year later on March 31, 1816.

23 John Wesley, "The Great Assize," *Works,* 5:183–85.

CHAPTER THREE:

The Just Shall Live by Faith

EVANGELICAL JUSTIFICATION

Preaching upon the text, "By grace are ye saved through faith," Wesley said that he "strongly enforced the first principles, which indeed never can be too much enforced."[1] He was referring to the doctrine of justification, or as it is affirmed in the Reformation motif, *sola fide*, justification by faith alone. When interpreted in the larger dimension of grace, faith and holiness, it lies at the heart of the Christian Gospel.

As used in Scripture, the words *justify* and *justification* normally have a forensic reference, closely related to the idea of trial and judgment (Deut. 25:1; 1 Kings 8:32; Matt. 12:37; Rom. 3:4; 1 Cor. 4:3). That is, one is justified when the demands of the law have been fully satisfied.

But how could this ever apply to us? No one is inherently righteous. We have all turned to our own way, transgressing the moral requirements of the holy law. Individually and corporately mankind has come under the just condemnation of sin and death.[2] Obviously from any standpoint of merit or innocence, we can not be justified before God.

Only in the Gospel sense of pardon can this term

apply to sinners. God simply by His own sovereign will forgives our sin for the sake of His Son who loved us unto death. In this figure, Christ is seen as the one altogether lovely taking unto Himself the judgment due to a fallen race. As our Representative, He assumed our legal liability when He suffered the consequence of our sin. The Father "made Him who knew no sin to be sin on our behalf, that we might become the righteousness of God in Him" (2 Cor. 5:21; cf. Gal. 3:13; Rom. 5:18).

By identification with the nature of His sacrificial act, the sinner is declared just and introduced into a state of righteousness. It is a decree from the high court of heaven establishing an entirely new relationship toward God. Both our relation to Him and His attitude toward us is changed through the Cross. God's nature is not changed; He is forever the same. But the way He looks at us is different. He sees us as we are in Christ (1 Cor. 1:30). In Him there is no condemnation (Rom. 8:1). The justified person thus stands before God free of all sin. "Therefore let it be known unto you, brethren, that through Him everyone who believes is freed from all things, from which you could not be freed through the law of Moses" (Acts 13:38–39).

SCRIPTURAL TERMINOLOGY

Imputation or *reckoning* is a term used to explain the way Christ's merit and character are ascribed to the sinner. The word means that the righteousness by which we are justified is not our own; it is Christ's and is accounted to the believer entirely by God's word of grace.

Paul cites Abraham's experience as an illustration of the principle. While Sarah was barren, God told Abraham that he would have a son, though empirical reason seemed to the contrary. Yet the old patriarch did not stagger at the promise of God, being fully persuaded that what God said he would also perform. "Therefore, it was reckoned to him as righteousness" (Rom. 4:22; cf. 3, 9, 23; Gal. 3:16; James 2:23; Gen. 15:6). Accordingly, Abraham was made the father of many nations "in the sight of Him whom he believed, even God, who gives life to the dead and calls into being that which does not exist" (Rom. 4:17). In the same way, we are to believe when the Gospel tells us that we have been made righteous in Christ, who "was delivered up for our transgressions, and was raised because of our justification" (Rom. 4:25).

Akin to this truth is the concept of *reconciliation*. Here the focus is upon bringing together two parties that were once separated. The sin that kept us apart is now removed, for "God was in Christ reconciling the world to Himself, not counting their trespasses against them" (2 Cor. 5:19). The resulting relationship is one of harmony and friendship. "Having made peace through the blood of His cross," we who were "formerly alienated and hostile in mind, engaged in evil deeds," He has now "reconciled in His fleshly body through death" (Col. 1:20–22).

The word *redemption* reflects much the same idea. As applied to us, it means to buy back and to set a prisoner free. Commonly the term in Jesus' day referred to the amount required to purchase the life of a slave; or in a slightly different rendering, it might be used in the context of ransom where a sum of money was supplied as the condition of release. Relating this concept to Christ's work, His blood is the purchase price of our redemption (1 Peter 1:18–19; Heb. 9:12; Eph. 1:7; Col. 1:14). Through His Cross we are ransomed from death and hell (Matt. 20:28; 1 Tim. 2:6). The shackles of sin are broken. Satan has lost his hold. There is a change of ownership. We belong now to Him who gave Himself for us. As Christ's bondslaves we are His treasured possession—His to keep, His to use, His to enjoy forever.

RELATION TO THE ATONEMENT

Running through all these terms is the vicarious sacrifice of Jesus Christ. He died in our place. We were all sold unto sin, under the sentence of death. But in God's amazing love, Jesus offered Himself as our Redeemer. The

life we now have in Christ is inseparable from His shed
blood on the cross.

Forgiveness through grace does not mean that God
mercifully overlooks sin as if it were of no consequence.
Such a view may have appeal to people who sentimentalize
God's nature of love, but it has no validity in Scripture. Sin
as the repudiation of God necessarily invokes His judgment. Anything that scorns His nature cannot be ignored.
Something must be done to remove the divine wrath
incurred because of sin.

How this can happen is represented by the term
propitiation. In pagan religions, it usually had reference to
what Romans could do to appease the offended deity.
However, when used in the Bible, it is God who takes the
initiative in removing His wrath. A gift is offered, but it is
God who offers it in Christ. He gives His blood. The gift is
pleasing to the Lord because it displays His own glory in
that He sacrifices His life for the creature of His love.[3]

Christ's blood changes the whole nature of our
salvation. God is seen as both the subject and the object of
propitiation. His wrath is removed, not because we do
anything, but because He did something. From beginning
to end, it is a display of His sovereign grace.

God hates evil, but He loves people. His love blazes
against that which would destroy His beloved—a love so
pure that it would not let us go even while we were yet
sinners. "In this is love, not that we loved God, but that He
loved us and sent His Son to be the propitiation for our
sins" (1 John 4:10; 2:2; Rom. 3:25). Through the Cross
God discloses His love in terms consistent with His justice
and holiness. By making Christ our Substitute, He satisfied
Himself while at the same time forgiving us.

WRONG VIEWS

Regrettably, this concept of substitution is often
ignored by modern theologians. Some relate it all to myth.[4]
A more common approach, however, is to interpret
Christ's death primarily as a revelation of love or self-

dedication. The sacrifice is not regarded as changing the relationship of God to man, but as furnishing the basis for an appeal to the sinner. The force of the Cross is directed manward, not Godward.[5] This moral influence idea, reminiscent of ancient Socinianism, runs through much of the teaching in Methodist churches today.[6]

Certainly the cross does reveal God's love, just as it discloses Christ's perfect obedience to the divine will. In recognizing this truth, however, we dare not minimize the satisfaction of divine justice through Christ's willing sacrifice on our behalf. John Wesley put it bluntly when he said, "If, as some teach, God never was offended, there was no need of this propitiation. And, if so, Christ died in vain."[7] The founders of Methodism, as the Reformers and the most revered Fathers of the church universal, have all recognized the full, complete, and perfect sacrifice of Christ for the sins of the whole world. Interpretations of the Atonement may be different, but at its heart is the objective fact that Calvary covers it all. The work is finished! Through His blood we have a new and living way into the very presence of God. Thus we can sing:

> Arise, my soul, arise;
> Shake off thy guilty fears:
> The bleeding Sacrifice
> In my behalf appears:
> Before the throne my Surety stands
> My name is written on His hands.
>
> He ever lives above,
> For me to intercede;
> His all-redeeming love,
> His precious blood, to plead:
> His blood atoned for all our race,
> And sprinkles now the throne of grace.[8]

NEW LIFE IN CHRIST

More than a change of relationship is ours in this new freedom. Persons dead in trespasses and sins not only die with Christ in the cross, but are raised in the power of His resurrection to walk in newness of life (Rom. 6:4). With justification comes regeneration of the human personality and adoption into the family of God. There is an actual change of character in the human heart through the impartation of the Holy Spirit. Justification may be viewed as Christ for us; regeneration may be described as Christ in us. Though different in nature, both belong to the miracle of conversion.

The Bible speaks of this transformation as a new birth, "born of the Spirit" (John 3:3–8); "born not of blood, nor of the will of the flesh, nor of the will of man, but of God" (John 1:13; cf. 1 John 3:9; 4:7). It is "a new creation; the old things pass away; behold, new things have come" (2 Cor. 5:17). The old corrupted self is laid aside, and a new self is put on, "which in the likeness of God has been created in righteousness and holiness of the truth" (Eph. 4:22–24).

Clearly something happens whereby the inner man is changed. This does not mean that God destroys human nature and ability. Rather He takes the natural powers of man and bends them to their true created purpose. In this sense, Christ enables us to fulfill our destiny as men and women created in the image of God (Col. 3:10–11). Only a person indwelt by His Spirit can live for real.

Renewed by this new principle within, the soul embraces and delights in the holiness of God. To the extent that the heart is controlled by the Spirit of Christ, the mind, the emotions, and the will act in conformity to the divine will. Love motivates life so that obedience to the law becomes a joy. The love of God in turn moves us to love our neighbor as we love ourselves. Spiritual perceptions are heightened, and with it a whole new system of values comes into focus. That which brings glory to God is seen now as the chief end of man.

It all centers in Christ whom the indwelling Spirit exalts within the believing heart; He is "all and in all" (Col. 3:11). There is fellowship with a personal Savior, a mystical union so real that Christ can be said to live in us and we in Him (John 15:4; cf. 14:20; Gal. 2:20; Col. 1:27; 3:4). Through His indwelling presence the fruits of the Spirit savor our lives with something of His own life quality (Gal. 5:22).

MOVING ON

Regeneration is only the beginning. Life in Christ is always moving "on toward the goal for the prize of the upward call of God" (Phil. 3:14), growing in "the knowledge of the Son of God, to a mature man, to the measure of the stature which belongs to the fullness of Christ" (Eph. 4:13). There is no end to it. Whatever we may have experienced heretofore, the best is yet to be. "Beholding as in a mirror the glory of the Lord," relentlessly we are "being transformed in the same image from glory to glory, just as from the Lord, the Spirit (2 Cor. 3:18).

This process of conformity to Christ is called sanctification. It means that God's Spirit is continuously working within our heart, setting apart a people for Himself. Like any surgical operation, the undertaking is not easy. There are times of suffering and pain. As understanding of God's will enlarges, misdirected areas of our present experience, including our carnal disposition of self-centeredness, must be brought into obedience to our Lord. But through it all, we may be assured that God is seeking our best interests. He intends to "present to Himself the church in all her glory, having no spot or wrinkle or any such thing; but that she should be holy and blameless" (Eph. 5:27).

The secret of this ever-expanding life in the fullness of the Spirit is simply to walk in the truth of God's Word. "If we walk in the light as He Himself is in the light, we have fellowship with one another, and the blood of Jesus His Son cleanses us from all sin" (1 John 1:7). This requires a daily yielding of our lives to His control. It is the attitude of perfect delight in the Father's will. Why should we fear? He never makes a mistake. And "all who are being led by the Spirit of God, these are the sons of God" (Rom. 8:14).

ASSURANCE OF SALVATION

There is no doubt about it! For in Christ we "have received a spirit of adoption as sons by which we cry out, Abba! Father!" (Rom. 8:15) This is not some supposition of hope, but a direct witness of the Spirit Himself with our spirits "that we are children of God" (Rom. 8:16). With all other members of His family, breathtaking as it may seem, we are now the "heirs of God and fellow-heirs with Christ" (Rom. 8:17).

Christians who do not rejoice in the assurance of their salvation are surely an anomaly to the New Testament church. For the Spirit testifies through the Word that our sins are forgiven—they are nailed to the cross (Col. 2:13–14). Delivered from the judgment of the law, we have peace with God (Rom. 5:1). Fear of the future is gone. The grave has lost its hold. We have already passed from death to life (John 5:24; 1 John 3:14). We do not know all the circuitous ways that our faith will be tested in this world, but we know whom we have believed, and are sure that He will keep that which is committed unto Him (2 Tim. 1:12). Come what may, we are more than conquerors through our victorious Lord. And nothing can separate us from His love (Rom. 8:37–39).

Little wonder that an air of celebration surrounds the apostolic witness. Just to think that we are united with Christ in an eternal bond of love—chosen in Him before the worlds were made (Eph. 1:4; 1 Peter 2:4). And whom God "foreknew, He also predestined to be conformed to the image of His Son" (Rom. 8:29; Eph. 1:5). In Him we "have obtained an inheritance," that we "should be to the praise of His glory" (Eph. 1:11–12). "He has made us to be a kingdom" (Rev. 1:6); "a chosen race, a royal priesthood" (1 Peter 2:9), possessing in Christ "every spiritual blessing in the heavenly places" (Eph. 1:3).

What more can we say? God is for us! His infinite desire to "freely give us all things" can be measured only by His sacrifice at Calvary (Rom. 8:32). Our finite minds cannot imagine the "breadth and length and height and depth" of such love. Yet, lost in its wonder, we can praise Him for His grace. And He "is able to do exceeding abundantly beyond all that we ask or think, according to the power that works within us" (Eph. 3:18–21).

GRACE AND FAITH

This life is entirely a gift of God, that is to say, it is not earned or acquired by human effort. As the Methodist Articles state, "the condition of man after the Fall of Adam, is such that he cannot turn and prepare himself, by his natural strength and works, to faith without the grace of God, by Christ preventing [i.e., preceding] us."[9] This is called prevenient grace.

Interestingly, when the *Discipline* of the Methodist Episcopal Church was revised at the General Conference of 1804, one preacher moved to strike out the word *preventing* from this Article, and insert in its place the word *assisting*. Superintendent Thomas Coke waited impatiently for the man to finish, then rose to his feet, and at the top of his voice exclaimed, "Where am I? In a Methodist Conference? I thought so, but have we turned Pelagians? Do we think that we can get along in our natural depravity with a little assistance, without preventing grace?" He insisted that the proposed amendment would ruin the intent of the Article which, as it stands, asserts the utter inability of anyone to do anything toward personal salvation except as God's grace through Christ prevents, or as the word means, "comes before." "Brethren," he cried, "Do not change the word. I would go to the stake, yes, to the stake, for that word, as soon as any word in the Bible."[10] Coke won his point, for the word was not changed, and, furthermore, it remains the same today.

Wesleyans teach that all have this enabling grace, and, therefore, every person *can* be saved. The elect are those persons who exercise this privilege and believe on Christ. Calvinists, on the other hand, hold that while everyone has common grace to enjoy a measure of goodness, only the foreordained elect for whom Christ died receive saving grace to embrace the Gospel. Of course, whether Arminian or Reformed in perspective, the only way to know if one is of the elect is to respond to the invitation of Christ. Without evangelism, then, neither system of thought has any practical validity; with it, either will be effective.[11]

Whatever one's theological position, the fact remains that "God so loved the world, that He gave His only begotten Son, that whoever believes in Him should not perish but have eternal life" (John 3:16). No other response to divine grace is expected. "As many as received Him, to them He gave the right to become children of God, even to those who believe in His Name" (John 1:12; cf. Acts 16:31; Heb. 10:39; Rom. 10:4).

By this is meant that the atoning sacrifice of Christ "once and for all" at Calvary is believed to be just that—it is offered and accepted as my own. Saving faith is not an intellectual consent to the credibility of His work nor a willingness for reformation of character; it is a complete reliance upon the Person of Jesus Christ, the Son of God, Who gave Himself for *me*.

Such faith, of course, is accompanied by repentance—a complete change of mind and purpose (Luke 13:3; Matt. 9:13; Rom. 2:4; 2 Tim. 2:25; 2 Peter 3:9). Until there is godly sorrow for sin and the willingness to turn from it, one may question how genuine faith is. It is academic as to which comes first. What needs emphasis is that repentance and faith are co-joined and flow together from the gracious working of the Holy Spirit. Penitent persons know that in their own merit they are nothing, and, confessing their guilt and corruption, cast themselves upon the mercies of God. In this feeling of helplessness and dependence we live thereafter determined to keep God's commandments.

Still it is God that makes it possible. From beginning to end redemption is the drama of *sola gratia*—grace alone. Resolution of amendment of life, noble deeds, high morality, fervent prayer, self-denial, sacramental rites— these good things are not unwanted by God; but finally nothing that we do ourselves can make us worthy of the

Savior's justifying act. We simply say yes to God's will. "For by grace you have been saved through faith; and that not of yourselves, it is the gift of God; not of works, that no one should boast" (Eph. 2:8–9).

THEOLOGICAL DISTINCTIONS

Theological friction between Protestants and Catholics becomes evident at this point. Official Roman doctrine asserts that justification comes partially through the infusion of supernatural grace at baptism. This has the effect of equating justification with sanctification, and allows to some degree divine bestowal of mercy because of what we are.[12] Justification thus is seen, not as a completed action, but as a gradual process through life; faith is only the first act; the believer is progressively made righteous as there is growth in sanctification. Not only does this view confound the biblical meaning of justification, but it also tends to make Christian growth the result of faith plus something else.

While evangelical Protestant theologians are agreed that salvation comes entirely by faith, there is an interesting difference between Calvinists and Arminians concerning its origin. Calvinists, following their view of the eternal decree, hold that the heart is "passive with respect to that act of the Holy Spirit whereby it is regenerated."[13] Only after the heart is awakened by God's exertion of creative power can the soul exercise saving faith. According to this position, a form of regeneration precedes justification, though in point of time it may be concomitant. This perspective stresses that regeneration is accomplished apart from human initiative, but it may also allow room for carelessness on the part of those who are not inclined to repent and obey the Gospel.

Arminians, on the other hand, believe that justification and regeneration are two sides of the same coin. It is contended that faith for righteousness is imputed by the grace of God, not the object of that faith. Such faith has no personal merit. Rather it is simply the free gift of God by which the righteousness of Christ is appropriated.

In fairness to all these views, no one wants to minimize the obligation to keep God's law. As James affirmed, "Faith, if it has no works, is dead" (James 2:17; cf. Matt. 25:34–46; Gal. 5:6). Even those like Luther, who had a hard time with this passage, still contend for faith expressing itself freely in obedience to the Word of God.[14] That we live entirely by grace in no way implies liberty to sin.

Something is wrong with any concept of justification that does not result in holiness of life. I must take exception to those who insist that justification may be completely hidden with no evidence of personal transformation and outgoing concern for others. Such a view would be in contradiction to God's redemptive purpose and creative power. Wesleyans, as the pietists and Puritans before them, rose as a protest to this kind of scholastic maneuvering. To use Wesley's words, "We know no Gospel without salvation from sin."[15]

A LIVING EXAMPLE

The relationship between justifying faith and transformation in Christ can be seen vividly in the experience of John Wesley. For years he had sought to know the reality of personal righteousness. Unsparingly he devoted himself to attain God's blessing through works of devotion and charity—he engaged in regular Bible study and prayer, entered into a small group to seek with others holiness of life, observed frequent attendance at Holy Communion, visited the sick and those in prison, gave generously of his means to the poor and naked, served as a minister of the Gospel at home and abroad—but all to no avail. He still had no assurance of salvation.

By the spring of 1738 Wesley was convinced that the cause of his "uneasiness was unbelief; and that the gaining of a true, living faith was the 'one thing needful.'"[16] Still, as he put it, "I fixed not this faith in its right object. I meant only faith in God, not faith in or through Christ. Again, I knew not that I was wholly void of this faith, but only thought I had not enough of it."[17]

However, his honest searching of the Scriptures and the supporting testimony of the confident Moravians finally resolved all his doubts. He became "thoroughly convinced that a true living faith in Christ is inseparable from a sense of pardon for all past and freedom from all present sins," that this faith was "the free gift of God; and that he would surely bestow it upon every soul who earnestly and perseveringly sought it."[18]

Significantly, when his quest ended at Aldersgate, a layman was reading from Luther's *Preface to the Epistle to the Romans,* which describes the change that God works in the heart through faith in Christ. Read for yourself some of the words John Wesley heard that day:

> The work of the law is everything that one does or can do, towards keeping the law of his own free will or by his own powers. But since under all these works and along with them there remains in the heart dislike for the law, and the compulsion to keep it, these works are all wasted and of no value. That is what St. Paul means when he says: "By the works of the law no man becomes righteous before God. . . ." To fulfill the law, however, is to do its works with pleasure and love, and to live a godly and good life of one's own accord, without the compulsion of the law. This pleasure and love for the law is put into the heart by the Holy Ghost. But the Holy Ghost is not given except in, with and by faith in Jesus Christ. And faith does not come save only through God's word or gospel, which preaches Christ, that he is God's Son and a man, and has died and risen again for our sakes. . . .
>
> Hence it comes that faith also makes righteous and fulfills the law; for out of Christ's merit it brings the Spirit, and the Spirit makes the heart glad and free as the law requires that it shall be. . . . Faith, however, is a divine work in us. It changes us and

makes us to be born anew of God (John 1); it kills
the old Adam and makes altogether new and
different men, in heart and spirit and mind and
powers, and it brings with it the Holy Ghost. O, it
is a living, busy, active, mighty thing, this faith,
and so it is impossible for it not to do good works
incessantly. It does not ask whether there are good
works to do, but before the question rises it has
already done them, and is always at the doing of
them. . . .

Faith is a living daring confidence in God's grace,
so sure and certain that a man would stake his life
on it a thousand times. This confidence in God's
grace, and knowledge of it, makes a man glad and
bold and happy in dealing with God and with all
his creatures; and this is the work of the Holy
Ghost in faith. Hence a man is ready and glad,
without compulsion, to do good to everyone, to
serve everyone, to suffer everything, in love and
praise to God, who has shown him this grace; and
thus it is impossible to separate works from faith,
as impossible as to separate heat and light from
fire.[19]

The compact between saving faith and experiential
righteousness could scarcely be stated more clearly. That
Wesley understood it is immediately apparent by the way
he began to pray fervently for his enemies, while also
openly testifying to the transformation felt in his heart.
There was no diminishing of good works, but now they
flowed out of love in grateful obedience to his Lord.

ALWAYS CONTEMPORARY

Modern churchmen may look wistfully to the witness
of John Wesley and lament that things are different in the
twentieth century. Ironically, Wesley thought the same
thing when Peter Böhler first tried to convince him of this
saving reality. Even when he was persuaded that it was the
teaching of the New Testament and the experience of the

early Christians, he argued, "Thus, I grant, God wrought in the first ages of Christianity; but times have changed. What reason have I to believe he works in the same manner now?" He was only "beat out of this retreat," he says, "by the concurring evidence of several living witnesses who testified God had thus wrought in themselves.[20]

His confrontation at Aldersgate erased all doubt. What the New Testament and the "living witnesses" had taught him now became a personal reality. Wesley's faith was lifted out of the realm of theory and established in the heart. The Gospel was not a mere creed; it was a living, throbbing, dynamic experience. To be sure, times had changed, but he found that the Gospel of God's redeeming love is forever the same. "The same resources that were available to the first Christians were available to him. And the same resources are available still for us, by the same grace of God and the same 'living, busy, active, mighty faith' of Paul, of Luther, of Peter Böhler and the Wesleys."[21]

This is the message of justification that is always contemporary. It is a doctrine that must be experienced in the present with every generation. How it happens, its manner and mode, the cultural pattern it reflects is inconsequential. All that matters is that salvation by faith in Jesus Christ become a living experience, and that in the radiance of this new life, we go forth to tell the world that Jesus saves.

> O that the world might know
> The all-atoning Lamb!
> Spirit of faith, descend and show
> The virtue of his Name:
> The grace which all may find,
> The Saving Power impart;
> And testify to all mankind,
> And speak in every heart.[22]

NOTES

[1] Wesley, *Works*, 4:399.

²On the essential fact that all persons are sinners, Arminian Wesleyans are as staunchly believers in original sin as orthodox Calvinists. In the language of the seventh Article of Religion, adopted from the Anglican Ninth Article, Methodists declare, "Original sin standeth not in the following of Adam (as the Pelagians do vainly talk), but it is the corruption of the nature of every man, that naturally is engendered by the offspring of Adam, whereby man is very far from original righteousness, and of his own nature inclined to evil, and that continually," Article VII, "Articles of Religion," *Discipline* (1988), 62; cf. Robert Emory, *History of the Discipline of the Methodist Episcopal Church* (New York: C. Lane and C.D. Tippett, 1845), 98.

³A competent study of this concept is John Stott's, *The Cross of Christ* (Downers Grove, Ill.: InterVarsity, 1986); Leon Morris', *The Apostolic Preaching of the Cross* (Grand Rapids: Eerdmans, 1955), 108–274; and Robert E. Coleman, *Written in Blood*, (Old Tappan, N. J.: Revell, 1972), 104–13.

⁴Rudolf Bultmann would typify this school. Note, e.g., his *Kerygma and Myth*, ed. H. W. Bartsch, trans. Reginald Fuller (New York: Harper, 1953), 7, 8, 35, 37.

⁵Eminent scholars like C. H. Dodd, D. M. Baillie and Vincent Taylor are typical of this position. An insightful summary of the views of these men may be found in the chapters by Robert Nicole, "The Nature of Redemption," and Lorman Peterson, "The Nature of Justification," in *Christian Faith and Theology*, ed. Carl F. H. Henry (New York: Channel, 1964), 193–221, 363–70.

⁶To the credit of the 1988 doctrinal statement of the *Discipline*, the new document on "Basic Christian Affirmations," while not elaborating on an objective vicarious atonement, still avoids the obvious leaning of the 1972 General Conference to the moral influence view. A comparison of the two statements reveals a slight move to a more evangelical position.

⁷John Wesley, *Explanatory Notes Upon the New Testament*, 530; cf. 531, 532, 536, 742, 801, 879, 905. Wesley does not labor to formulate any particular theory of the Atonement, but he consistently affirms the fact that "the offering of Christ, once made, is that perfect redemption, propitiation, and satisfaction for all the sins of the whole world," Article XX, "The Articles of Religion," *Discipline* (1988), 66.

⁸Charles Wesley, from the hymn "Arise, My Soul, Arise."

⁹Article VIII, *Discipline*, 63.

¹⁰Quoted in C. Elliott, *The Life of the Rev. Robert B. Roberts* (Cincinnati: J. F. Wright and L. Formstedt, 1844), 121–22.

¹¹As to the theoretical side of election and predestination, one can enter into a heated debate. To get an idea of John Wesley's strong feeling on the issue, read his sermon, "On Free Grace," *Works*, 7:373–86. A scholarly discussion of this whole doctrine is Allan Coppedge's,

John Wesley in Theological Debate (Wilmore, Ky.: Wesley Heritage Press, 1987).

[12] *The Catholic Bible Encyclopedia* defines righteousness as "the permanent state of those who are inherently righteous (just) or inwardly sanctified, because through the merits of Jesus Christ they have been justified by the real remission of their sins as well as by a true inward renewal and sanctification wrought by sanctifying grace intrinsically inhering in the soul" (New York: Joseph F. Wagner, 1955), 552.

[13] A. A. Hodge, *Outlines of Theology* (Grand Rapids: Zondervan, 1972, c. 1860), 460.

[14] There is considerable difference of opinion regarding Luther's position on justification and the resulting life of obedience. Some scholars, like Karl Hall, contend that Luther believed justification involved actual moral transformation of a sinner into a saint. Approaching the justification of man analytically, he held that God's judgment is viewed eschatologically on the basis of what man shall become. Theologians, like Barth, take strong exception to this interpretation, believing that it is little different than the Roman Catholic teaching. The problem centers in subjectivizing the act of God's grace. However, this does not have to be the case, it seems to me, if the norm of God's truth in Jesus Christ is kept clearly in focus. Perhaps it would be best not to strain the basic forensic sense of justification, but to note the inseparable relation of justifying faith to regeneration and sanctification. Note the discussion of this issue in G. C. Berkouwer, *Faith and Justification* (Grand Rapids: Eerdmans, 1954), 9–22.

[15] Wesley, *Letters* 6:326.

[16] Wesley, *Journal* 1:471.

[17] Ibid.

[18] Ibid.

[19] Martin Luther, *Works of Martin Luther*, 30 vols., (Philadelphia: Muhlenberg, 1932), 6:449–52.

[20] Wesley, *Journal* 1:454–55.

[21] Philip S. Watson, *The Message of the Wesleys* (New York: MacMillan, 1964), 18.

[22] Charles Wesley, from the hymn "Spirit of Faith, Come Down."

CHAPTER FOUR:

The Mandate of Holiness

MAKING DISCIPLES OF CHRIST

Off the coast of Scotland is a little island where Christianity first took root in the nation. To accommodate the many tourists who want to make the trip across the bay to visit the historic site, there is a rental shop on the mainland where transportation can be obtained. Over the door of the small building, emblazoned in bold letters, is the signboard: "VISIT THE HOLY ISLE." Then, more to the point, underneath are the words: "WE CAN TAKE YOU."

In a much more profound sense, those last words express what the church should be doing—taking people where the saints have trod. In practical terms, this means bringing men and women into the deeper and ever-expanding dimensions of holiness.

Such a ministry does not for a moment minimize the necessity of conversion, for the kingdom life cannot be entered until one is born of the Spirit. But the mandate of Christ is not to make converts, but to "make disciples"— followers of Jesus—persons who will develop into the likeness of the Master (Matt. 28:19–20). Herein is the genius of His plan of world evangelization. For disciples of

Christ grow into the character of their Lord, and thereby become involved in His mission. Mature disciples thus become disciplers of others, and as they in turn make disciples, through the process of reproduction, a church someday will be gathered from every tongue and tribe and nation.[1]

John Wesley focused this strategy of the Great Commission in his charge to the preachers, not only to bring sinners to repentance, but "to build them up in that holiness without which they cannot see the Lord."[2] He was of the conviction that no one should "dream of going to heaven by any faith that does not produce holiness."[3]

Echoing this basic tenet of the Wesleyan revival, John McClintock, who was to become the first president of Drew Theological School, fervently declared in a Methodist centenary service in 1867:

> Our work is a moral work; that is to say, the work of making men holy. Our preaching is for that, our church agencies are for that, our schools, colleges, universities and theological seminaries are for that. There is our mission—there is our glory—there is our power, and there shall be the ground of our triumph. God keep us true.[4]

HOLINESS IN MISSION

One hopes that what is affirmed in these words is not the triumphalism of a church asserting her superior piety, as has been sometimes alleged.[5] Rather, it is the announcement of persons, overwhelmed with the knowledge of redeeming grace, that the Lord Almighty, of purer eyes than to behold evil, wants to make a people to display His glory: "You shall be holy, for I am holy" (1 Peter 1:16; cf. Lev. 11:45). If there is any boasting, it cannot be by virtue of any righteousness inherent in the saints, but only that they belong to Him who loved them and died for their sin.

This sense of divine ownership through the blood of Christ lies at the heart of holiness. The terms *saint* and *sanctify* come from the same root, meaning to set apart or to be God's possession.

Certainly this state cannot be claimed as the exclusive property of Methodism or any other favored body of believers. Holiness, as the reflection of the divine nature, is the fabric of all Christian experience, though called by different names.

The manifestation of this character has been the basis of God's program to reach the world. The commission comes into bold announcement when Abraham was called to leave the old haunts of sin and go out with his Lord by faith (Gen. 12:1–3; cf. Heb. 11:8–10). To this end Israel was chosen to be His witness among the nations, that people beholding their holy manner of life would want to follow their God (Zech. 8:23; Isa. 55:4–5; Jer. 10:7; Pss. 2:8; 46:10). When the Jews succumbed to the sensate culture about them, the Lord sent His Messiah-Son to raise up a new Israel, a holy nation, of which His life was witness (Isa. 49:6; 53:11–12; Gen. 49:10; Zech. 9:10; Dan. 7:13–14). The Spirit now is fashioning the church in that image in order to show the glory of God to the ends of the earth (Acts 1:8; cf. Rev. 4:9–10; 7:9).

TO BE LIKE CHRIST

It is this likeness of Christ in the saints that makes holiness beautiful. Worldlings can see that persons who bear His name are different. There is a graciousness about their lifestyle; a humility of servanthood that finds expression in deeds of love. Precept and example blend together in authentic witness. Obedience is joyful. Even amid sufferings, when ridiculed and oppressed, the bitterness of the world does not keep the saints from praising God from whom all blessings flow. Such a life creates a mystery; it is so utterly uncharacteristic of a fallen race, and those who are most observing, just like the church-watchers of the apostolic era, have to admit that His disciples have "been with Jesus" (Acts 4:13, KJV). The print of His character is upon them.

That is what sanctification is all about. It transforms disciples of Christ into his image, "from glory to glory, even as by the Spirit of the Lord" (2 Cor. 3:18, KJV). This is no outward show of good works, least of all some kind of legalistic code of religious behavior. Nor can it be equated with any manifestation of a particular spiritual gift. The focus of holiness is always Jesus Christ; He is the Word made flesh, whom the Spirit glorifies (John 16:5–16). The only holiness we can know is in relationship to His.

This character does not make one immune to the beguiling enticements of Satan nor does it cause one to escape the persecutions that come for righteousness' sake. Indeed, by following Christ, we may expect to encounter some difficulties in our pagan environment that might otherwise be avoided. Let no one imagine that sanctity exempts humanity from the realities of this fallen age.

PURITY OF DESIRE

Moreover, unlike the Lord who had no inherent sin, saints have to contend all through life with their own depraved minds. Though education can correct some consequences of a darkened intelligence, despite these efforts at learning, holy people are going to make decisions unbecoming to the nature of Christ. That is part of our human situation. Notwithstanding these limitations, however, a holy desire to please the Lord can still shine through the life of His saints.

An experience with my son many years ago illustrates what I mean. It was a hot day at the end of the harvest season. Jim, who was then no more than three or four years old, saw me working, and it occurred to him that I might be thirsty. So he pulled a chair up to the kitchen sink, found a dirty glass, and filled it with water from the faucet. The next thing I knew my name was being called. As I turned around, there was my son coming across the garden holding that smudgy glass of warm water, and saying, "Daddy, I thought you were thirsty so I brought you a drink." And, as he held up the glass, a smile stretched across his face from one ear to the other.

You might think, "Couldn't he do better than that? Why, that is not cool water; that's not even pure water." And you would be right. But when you look at his face, you have to say that that is pure love. He was doing the best he knew to please his daddy.

In some similar way, that is how every Christian can live in this world. Though we continually make errors in judgment and fall woefully short of our desire to be like Christ, still in our hearts we can do the best we know to please Him.

PERFECT LOVE

Herein is the essence of what Wesley called "Christian perfection." It is not a maturity in knowledge or in attainment, but a "purity of intention," so that "one desire or design" rules the affections.[6] To the question, "How shall we avoid setting perfection too high or low?" he answered:

> By keeping to the Bible, and setting it just as high as the Scripture does. It is nothing higher and nothing lower than this,—the pure love of God and man; the loving God with all our heart and soul, and our neighbor as ourselves. It is love governing the heart and life, running through all our tempers, words, and actions.

In this expectation he was only echoing the Great Commandment (Matt. 22:37–40), which becomes the constraining force of the Great Commission (2 Cor. 5:14). Such love is holy because it is of God—His own nature infused in the heart of His people by the Spirit of Christ (Rom. 5:5; 1 John 4:7–8, 16).

Firmly convinced that this was the substance of every moral obligation of Scripture, John Wesley did not hesitate to make it the "grand depositum" of his teaching.[8] Seen in its "own shape," he asked, "Who will fight against it?"

Indeed, "it must be disguised before it can be opposed."[9] Then in the words of the prayer so often heard in church, he affirmed, "Yea, we do believe, that He will in this world so 'cleanse the thoughts of our hearts, by the inspiration of his Holy Spirit, that we shall perfectly love him, and worthily magnify his holy name.' "

SIN UNDERSTOOD AS CONTINUING

The question might be asked, though, whether this devotion is the common experience of everyone at the time one is born of the Spirit, or whether it is a commitment disciples come to in the process of sanctification. At this point, different answers are forthcoming, depending upon the theological system in which holiness is cast. Unfortunately, most of us tend to view sainthood so much through the glasses of our own tradition that we fail to appreciate how others, using different-colored lenses, see it. Basically these variances of perspective settle along the lines of Calvinism on the one hand and Arminianism on the other—positions that solidify in the churches they represent.

Much of the condition could be resolved by a better understanding of terms, particularly the way sin is defined. In the Reformed tradition, of which Calvin would be chief spokesman, sin is seen as any deviation from the absolute holiness of God, whether it is realized or not. No allowance is made for human infirmities over which we have little control, like ignorance, a weak physical body, hereditary handicaps, psychological quirks going back to childhood, and a lot of other involuntary human traits. Obviously from this perspective, everyone comes short of the standard of righteousness in Christ, whatever the person's state of grace. To do otherwise would require perfect knowledge with no residue of human depravity. So far as any experience of absolute holiness on this earth is concerned, it would be blasphemy to speak of being free from sin. The only sense in which this could be allowed is from the vantage point of heaven, where, because of identity with the Son by faith, God imputes to saints the righteousness of Christ. Complete experiential sanctification, however, must await the day when believers are delivered from a corrupted body in glorification.

By keeping clear the infinite perfection of the Lord, this position makes us ever mindful of our human failing in the flesh, even as it points us to the endless possibilities of improvement. Also, as an unrelenting judge of superficiality in Christian experience, it should help us with humility. John Wesley appreciated this viewpoint, and taking a cue from the Westminster Catechism, made it a practice to confess continually those unconscious sins committed against the divine Majesty in "thought, word, and deed," a custom still followed by Methodists every time we take holy Communion.[11]

HOLINESS IN A SINLESS PERSPECTIVE

But in terms of transgression of the known will of God, Wesley, reflecting an Arminian perspective, believed that it is possible by grace to live blamelessly in this present life. He could make this claim because of his differentiation between sins of intent and sins of ignorance or mistakes. A sin of intent is a wrong choice issuing from an unholy motive. A mistake is a wrong choice issuing from a holy motive. This does not make the mistaken action any less short of God's perfection nor does it absolve the sinner from the consequence resulting from the transgression, but it does allow that the heart is condemned only for willful disobedience.[12]

Within this framework Wesley also made a distinction between traits of the fallen human nature and the willful carnal nature of self-centeredness. Since after regeneration human infirmities remain in the physical body, obviously, at best, fleshly characteristics can only be restrained or counterbalanced. But that selfish carnal disposition sapping spiritual vitality need not be endured, since it exists by our permission. When recognized, like any volitional perversion, it can be confessed and cleansed.

Admittedly, this delicate distinction between the involuntary and deliberate aspects of sin may be difficult to apply in practice. After all, can one ever be sure that he or she has utilized every privilege of grace to know the mind of Christ? In this regard slothfulness in seeking the truth can be deceptive. No wonder Calvinists look askance at our claims. But in theory, at least, the Wesleyan perspective offers an expedient for believing that an obedient disciple, in standing before God as well as in personal experience, can be free of conscious condemnation.

When this basic difference in the definition of sin is understood, there is no reason why Calvinists and Wesleyans cannot agree on the essential character of a holy life.[13] Our terminology explaining justification and sanctification, of necessity, will differ, but we can embrace the same reality.[14]

Perhaps, in divine providence, both of these foundational evangelical systems of thought are given support in Scripture to make all of us more sensitive to our own finite inability to comprehend "with all the saints what is the breadth, and length, and depth, and height, and to know the love of Christ which surpasses knowledge" (Eph. 3:18–19). I suspect that in the end we will discover that God does not value our definitions of theology nearly so much as He does a broken and contrite spirit.

ENTIRE SANCTIFICATION

Both Calvinists and Arminians believe that the condition for full salvation is simple faith in the finished work of Jesus Christ. In terms of consciousness, this means offering all that we know of ourselves to all that we know of Him. Such commitment begins at conversion and continues throughout life as we walk "not after the flesh, but after the Spirit" (Rom. 8:1, KJV).

What is sometimes called "entire sanctification," as the compound word in I Thessalonians 5:23 may be translated, is a term that points to a particular moment in the developing life of grace when carnality is confronted.

While it involves a definite confrontation with truth in relation to the self-life, it is only a part of the ongoing sanctifying process. However, because the nature of this point in Christian obedience requires the deepest commitment of the will, the decision it forces for many stands out as a monumental crisis. With others the decision may come so gradually, interwoven with so many other things, that knowledge of its reality may be only the quiet assurance that it's settled. What matters is not the manner of the submission, nor any accompanying sign, but the release from the bondage of self it brings.

For Wesleyans who interpret this experience as the cleansing of the carnal mind, distinguishing it from the ever-present human nature, it is sometimes referred to as a "second work of grace." The expression is not meant to depreciate the grace already received. Rather it is a recognition that when a saint is able to see the conflict caused by self-centeredness and is willing to surrender the problem to God, the Spirit, who is already working in one's life, can also meet this deeper need.[15]

CONTINUAL GROWTH

Many problems will have to be faced in the growing experience of holiness. Some of these issues will occasion very real spiritual battles, but in meeting them, the saint can draw upon the strength of a heart fully yielded to the will of God.

It is a commitment that must be continually renewed, for everything that comes up—in the family, at school, on the job—everything involves holiness. For this reason, it would be better not to think of cleansing as a crisis but as a life. The life is made up of a constant series of decisions, and how each one is made will determine the blessedness of holiness.

Surely endless corrections will be called for as persons being sanctified seek to follow the Lord. Renouncing our own rights and taking up His cross has implications in prayer and service of which we may have only faint comprehension now, but the Spirit will be faithful to bring them to our attention as we seek His guidance. As moral failure is perceived, we must confess the sin and align our wills with the sanctifying Word.

Thanks be to God, there is never a foreclosure on progress. No matter what has been experienced thus far, there is more to learn. As the character of life in Christ is more fully understood and faith enlarges to embrace it, there will be unceasing expansion in the Spirit's fullness, even as life lengthens into the timeless dimensions of eternity.

The goal is nothing less than the very perfection of our Savior. While it remains ever a vision infinitely beyond our experience, it is nevertheless a glorious incentive to press on to higher ground, reaching always "toward the mark for the prize of the high calling of God in Christ Jesus" (Phil. 3:14, KJV). If we are growing in faith, the closer we get to the heavenly city, the more our soul will long to see His face.

KEEPING HOLINESS IN FOCUS

In view of the unspeakable blessing of this life of divine grace, one would think that the body of saints would constantly herald the beauty of holiness. Yet, strangely, this does not seem to be the case. Not that the truth is denied; it is just that other things appear to be more appealing, and the church under the illusion of relevance, tends to accept the world's agenda of concerns. Inevitably, then, more mundane and humanitarian interests take precedent over the demanding claims of the lordship of Christ.

We would not expect persons coming from a Reformed communion, of course, to speak with integrity of sanctification in the same manner as Wesleyans. As already noted, they have their own structure in which to place the doctrine, and we should encourage them to say it their way. In my own experience, when holiness is explained in their context, using a biblical frame of reference, I have found generally a warm and grateful response. Of course, if our Calvinist friends have any reason to suspect that we do not cherish the Bible as the inspired Word or if they detect in us a shallow treatment of the Text, we will probably not experience a meeting of the minds.

In this respect, whether the audience be Reformed or Arminian, the presentation of sanctification will be considerably enhanced by a careful exposition of Scripture. I am afraid that in Wesleyan circles, to our shame, far too much emphasis has been given to the recitation of personal testimonies to the neglect of solid biblical exegesis. This deficiency is one reason, I am convinced, holiness teaching so often is compromised.

Human experiences help to illustrate the power of the written Word, but only the authoritative Book of God can focus the full reality of holiness. The muting of this central truth of Scripture in the private and public witness of the church, whatever the tradition, reflects a tragic displacement of priorities.

DANGER IN A DEFENSIVE POSTURE

Bound up with this confusion is an inordinate fear of fanaticism, which, unfortunately, some misguided people associate with holiness. Just the thought of this message conjures in their minds images of wild emotionalism or antisocial behavior. Please do not misunderstand. I am not suggesting that we should endorse every harebrained zealot who crowds under the holiness umbrella, for clearly there are many strange fellow-travelers. But this is something over which we have scant jurisdiction. If making disciples of Christ is indeed a militant movement, like any advancing army, our flanks will always be vulnerable to aberrations. Let us be careful, however, that in our desire to be removed from these perceived excesses, we do not become defensive and divert our energy from the attack. Whatever the misrepresentations and the criticisms that they may invoke, the church must not be intimidated into fighting a holding action.

It seems to me this is a failing all too common today in the so-called "holiness movement." Too much time is expended to protect ourselves from embarrassment—pointing out that we are not this and we are not that, until I almost get the impression that we are more astute in maintaining an appearance of respectability than we are confident in our own experience.

Our call is not to hold the fort but to storm the heights. Anytime we become more concerned with self-preservation than with proclamation, we have lost our advantage in the mission of Christ. True holiness needs no defense; it will vindicate itself when seen in its own beauty.

RESISTANCE OF THE FLESH

This is not to say that the holy life will elicit popular acceptance from the masses. For by its nature, holiness will always have an uphill battle with the flesh, since it cuts across the grain of the carnal mindset. If we are overly sensitive to what people think, we will never do much preaching of holiness.

It should not seem surprising, for this reason, that in Wesley's day there were among his followers many who "little insisted on" this message.[16] The same problem will be seen in Francis Asbury's travels, when he noted that "sanctification and Christian perfection" were not "commonplace subjects"—a fact, incidentally, that caused him to resolve to "make them the savor of every sermon" he preached.[17]

The situation is aptly described by Benjamin Lakin, an itinerant Methodist minister, who made the following entry in his diary under the date March 15, 1814:

> I have been making some inquiry into the cause of the gloom that is on the minds of professors and the decline of religion. Lately an old Brother observed that he had observed for some time our preaching to begin with the fall of man, the redemption of Jesus Christ, repentance and justification by faith, and here we stopped, and for a

long time he had not heard the doctrine of sanctification enforced. I immediately began to make my observation on experiences that I hear, and for a considerable time have observed them go as far as justification and there stop and no talk of sanctification. I have further observed that professors have lost that bright experience (at least too many of them) of their acceptance with God they once had, and rest too much on general determinations to serve God. And as I have reason to thank God that there is as little immoral conduct among us as I could expect among so large a body, I concluded the following causes have produced this effect: (1) The confused state of affairs and the interest every man takes in the event of war, (2) We have preached the gospel but have been deficient in enforcing the doctrine of sanctification, and (3) the people stopped in a justified state without pursuing holiness. Immediately I set about a reform in myself, and began to preach and enforce the doctrine of holiness by showing the state I found the people to be in, and the need of perfecting holiness in the fear of God.[18]

HOLINESS IN CHURCH GROWTH

What can be detected in this faithful circuit rider's account underscores the continuing need for renewal of our first love if the priorities of the kingdom are to be maintained. This becomes increasingly imperative in succeeding generations of any revival movement, of which Methodism is a prime example. By and large, the holiness teaching of Wesley became diluted, as well as slighted, as the nineteenth century progressed and the doctrine of entire sanctification met with increasing resistance from the hierarchy of the church. The tensions from this conflict, in combination with other conditions, resulted in the formation of various new holiness denominations and contributed to the rise of the modern Pentecostal movement.[19]

Many stalwart exponents of the holiness doctrine

remained in the establishment, but, bereft of institutional support, their influence in shaping policy of mainline Methodism has been marginal for more than a hundred years. The loss of this emphasis has been progressively apparent in the ministry of the church, of which the erosion of evangelistic effectiveness and the corresponding membership decline is only one symptomatic evidence. On the other hand, the dissident holiness groups imbued with a revival spirit, many of which came out of Methodism, generally have manifested a higher degree of commitment and, as a by-product, a sustained increase of disciples.

There are numerous factors to consider in church growth, of course, but among them certainly must be included a shared quest for heart holiness. Whenever this scriptural truth has been lifted up in word and deed, beginning with the apostles, the blessing of God has been obvious in evangelism, despite buffetings of the world. Any time this principle of growth is compromised, while not immediately apparent, degeneration inevitably follows in the long term.

WEAKNESS OF CONTEMPORARY METHODISM

Here, I believe, is a glaring fallacy in much of the talk today about church growth. It is simply too shallow to develop the necessary spiritual resources for dynamic reproduction. Attention seems to center more on better sociological understanding, better programs of outreach, better training in management, and the like, all of which are helpful. But the great theological and spiritual issues in sanctification are largely ignored. Ecclesiastical rhetoric is confused with godliness.

All of us saw the popular television commercial of several years ago that featured a haggard old lady looking at a hamburger. With an expression of bewilderment on her face, she asked the server in the fast-food restaurant, "Where's the beef?" Her predicament is somewhat analogous to the feeling of persons looking for the substance of the Wesleyan revival in our churches today. Where is the "beef" of holiness, that ingredient of Christian experience that Wesley described as "religion itself"?[20] For that matter, I have to confess that even in institutions founded to propagate holiness I have sometimes wondered where the unabashed, forthright witness is to this most distinctive of Methodist doctrines. Oh, yes, one can recognize references here and there—code words like "second blessing" or "perfect love"—intended to convey an association with the tradition. But upon closer examination so often it turns out that the hamburger is mostly a bun.

FACING UP TO CARNALITY

Why is this? Why do holy people, and the institutions they build, drift away from the holiness mandate? Doubtless there are many reasons, but the heart of the problem, I believe, is the pervasive tendency of the flesh to take the course of least resistance. Call it what you may, unless this human characteristic is persistently overcome through the renewing power of the Holy Spirit, the deceitful nature of carnality, ever lurking in the shadows of disobedience, will arise stealthily to take control. Consent to its leavening influence may be so gradual and refined as to be undetected at first, and when it is detected, it will likely seem normal. After all, do we not need times to relax and enjoy the pleasures of the world? Do we always have to bear the cross of Christ? Why should we have to bring the Great Commission into every aspect of our lifestyle?

Such questions may seem innocent enough, but carnality has a beguiling way of turning our response into self-indulgence. All too easily we pamper ourselves under the guise of God's blessing, failing to measure our life by the pattern of our Lord. This inclination is but the flesh lusting against the spirit, traits of the "old man" underlying the attitudes seen in the classical seven deadly sins—lust, envy, anger, pride, gluttony, avarice, sloth.[21] However we may try to ignore the deeper problem of self-centeredness, it is there to frustrate, if not to defeat a victorious life.

Holiness is an exacting standard, and as the values of Christ's kingdom become clearer, the more we will identify with the publican when he cried, "Lord, have mercy on me!" Quibbling over hair styles and forms of dress will not be the issue. But when seeing ourselves with more Christlikeness, I suspect that we will become far more sensitive in such areas as worldliness, materialism, prayerlessness, disregard of the oppressed, and indifference to the lost multitude that has never heard the gospel.

Here we must be utterly honest with ourselves, and with God's help relentlessly seek day by day to bring our lives into conformity with His holiness. If we try to trim the corners and excuse a few favorite shortcomings, carnality reigns in our hearts. As long as this condition exists, we diminish the blessing of holiness to others.

THE INCONTROVERTIBLE WITNESS

Would it be fair to ask about any evidence of sainthood people see in your life? Finally, is this not where the issue rests with us all?

A dear friend of mine, when being examined for admission into a United Methodist Conference, was asked by the Board of the Ordained Ministry, "Are you wholly sanctified?" Detecting a spirit of skepticism, yet wanting to be helpful, he replied, "Don't you think that you are asking the wrong person? My wife is sitting outside in the lobby. Why don't you talk to her?"

What a Solomonic response! Could you imagine a better way to put this doctrine to the test? It's not the creed we profess that convinces other persons of holiness; it's the life they see.

I will never forget the closing service of the World Congress on Evangelism in the great Kongresshalle in Berlin, West Germany, in 1966. Billy Graham was speaking on the need in Christian work for "a gentleness and a kindness and a love and a forgiveness and a compassion that will mark us as different from the world." He said, "The Christian minister is to be a holy man."[22]

Then to illustrate his point he told the story of the conversion of Dr. H. C. Morrison, founder of Asbury Theological Seminary. He described a day many years ago when Morrison as a farm worker was cultivating in a field. Looking down the road, he saw an old Methodist circuit rider coming by on his horse. The young plowman had seen the preacher before, and he knew him to be a holy man. As he watched the saint go by, he felt the power of his godly presence way out there in the field. Such a sense of conviction for sin came over Morrison, that fearful for his soul, he dropped on his knees, and there between the corn rows, alone, he made a resolve to give his life to God.

As he concluded the story, Billy Graham, earnestly prayed, "Oh, God, make me a holy man—a holy man."[23]

That is the prayer, I trust, that bespeaks the yearning of all our souls. Upon its answer is the hope of revival in the church.

NOTES

[1] For a biblical development of this concept, see my books, *The Master Plan of Evangelism* and *The Master Plan of Discipleship* (Old Tappan, N. J.: Revell, 1964, 1987).

[2] Wesley, "Minutes of Several Conversations," *Works*, 8:310.

[3] Wesley, *Works*, 4:95.

[4] Quoted by Timothy Smith, *Revivalism and Social Reform* (Nashville: Abingdon, 1957), 137. Interestingly, in this same address, Dr. McClintock described holiness as "the great central idea of the whole book of God." He went on to say, "It may be called fanaticism, but that, dear friend, is our mission. If we keep to that, the next century is ours."

[5] Douglas Frank, for example, in his book *Less Than Conquerors, How Evangelicals Entered the Twentieth Century* (Grand Rapids: Eerdmans, 1986), suggests that persons at the turn of the century who were seeking to propagate holiness associated with perfectionism, were "drunk on their own power . . . confusing it with the power of God" (p. 27). Though his study of holiness teaching centers primarily on the "victorious-life" theology of the Keswick Movement, coming more out of a Reformed background, what he says also pertains to the Wesleyan emphasis of the same period. His major concern seems to be with a perceived arrogance and pride in this stream of evangelicalism, which he blames, along with dispensational premillennialism and revivalism, for the present superficiality in the church. What he fails to comprehend is

that the holiness movement in its various forms for more than a century has never really dominated the mainstream of Christendom in America. The lack of a self-effacing, suffering attitude that Dr. Frank has observed in evangelicalism in general may have some basis in fact, and we can appreciate the warning he gives; but I feel that his assessment of the "deeper life" or "perfectionism," even his treatment of revivalism, leaves much to be desired.

[6] Wesley, *A Plain Account of Christian Perfection, Works,* 11:444.

[7] Ibid., 397.

[8] Letter to Robert Carr Brackenbury, September 15, 1790, *Letters,* 8:238. Referring to his delight with regard to "full sanctification," Wesley in this letter said, "This doctrine is the grand depositum which God has lodged with the people called Methodists; and for the sake of propagating this chiefly He appeared to have raised us up."

[9] Wesley, *A Plain Account of Christian Perfection, Works,* 11:445f.

[10] Ibid., 445–46.

[11] *The Westminster Shorter and Larger Catechism,* in *The Confession of Faith of the Presbyterian Church in the United States Together with the Larger Catechism and the Shorter Catechism* (Richmond: John Knox, 1964), 330, 428. Cf. Prayer of General Confession in the Order for the Administration of the Sacrament of the Lord's Supper, The United Methodist Church. It should be noted that since Wesley believed that there is no perfection in this life that excludes involuntary transgressions, he said, "Sinless perfection is a phrase I never use, lest I should seem to contradict myself." *A Plain Account of Christian Perfection, Works,* 11:396.

[12] It should not be assumed from this position that persons who have never heard the Gospel are excused from the consequences of rejecting Christ. For Wesley, in classical evangelical reasoning, insisted that sufficient direction comes through natural revelation to make everyone accountable. Those who have not had opportunity to sit under the preaching of the Word, thus, still must answer for their chosen way of iniquity.

[13] A helpful treatment of major Protestant approaches to this subject is the book, *Five Views on Sanctification* (Grand Rapids: Zondervan, 1987). In this volume, the Wesleyan position is treated by Melvin E. Dieter; the Reformed view by Anthony A. Hoekema; the Pentecostal understanding by Stanley M. Horton; the Keswick position by J. Robertson McQuilkin; and the Augustinian-Dispensational approach by John F. Walvoord. While the distinctives of each position are defended, it is interesting how these major schools of thought coalesce around the necessity of Christians living a holy life. From the standpoint of a deeper sense of sanctification subsequent to conversion, read how various leaders in different Protestant traditions describe their own experiences in the book by V. Raymond Edmon, *They Found the Secret* (Grand Rapids: Zondervan, 1984, 1960).

[14] This would be especially true of Wesleyans and Calvinists of a Keswick orientation. As J. Robertson McQuilkin, writing from this perspective, states, "If the ambiguous terms are defined in a particular way, Wesleyan teaching and the Keswick approach are quite compatible. If sin is falling short of God's glorious character, no one is perfect. Yet, every Spirit-empowered believer may consistently refrain from deliberately violating God's known will." *Five Views on Sanctification*, 55.

[15] A simple Bible study focused on this doctrine is the author's, *The Spirit and the Word* (Wilmore, Ky.: Christian Outreach, 1968). For a more complete theological treatment, see Harald Lindström, *Wesley and Sanctification: A Study in the Doctrine of Salvation* (Grand Rapids: Zondervan/Francis Asbury Press, 1983); W.T. Purkiser, *Exploring Christian Holiness*, 3 vols. (Kansas City: Beacon Hill, 1986); and Laurence W. Wood, *Pentecostal Grace* (Grand Rapids: Zondervan/Francis Asbury Press, 1984).

[16] *Letters* 4:149. In this letter Wesley went on to observe that when such neglect was common "there is little increase, either in the numbers or the grace of the hearers."

[17] Asbury, *Journal*, Monday, March 1, 1803, quoted in *Francis Asbury's America*, compiled and edited by Terry D. Bilhartz (Grand Rapids: Zondervan/Francis Asbury Press, 1984), 82.

[18] Benjamin Lakin, *Journal*, in William Warren Sweet, *Religion on the American Frontier*, 4 vols. *The Methodists, 1783–1840, A Collection of Source Materials* (Chicago: University of Chicago Press, 1946), 4:249.

[19] A chronicling of this history will be found in Melvin E. Dieter, *The Holiness Revival of the Nineteenth Century* (Metuchen, N.J.: Scarecrow, 1980); John Leland Peters, *Christian Perfection and American Methodism* (Grand Rapids: Zondervan//Francis Asbury Press, 1984); and Donald W. Dayton, *Theological Roots of Pentecostalism* (Grand Rapids: Zondervan/Francis Asbury Press, 1987).

[20] "Our main doctrines," wrote Wesley, "which include all the rest, are repentance, faith and holiness. The first of these we account, as it were, the porch of religion; the next, the door; the third, religion itself." Letter to Thomas Church, June 17, 1746, *Letters*, 2:268.

[21] For a modern treatment of these conditions, see Anthony Campolo, *Seven Deadly Sins* (Wheaton, Ill.: Victor, 1987).

[22] Billy Graham, "Stains on the Altar." *One Race, One Gospel, One Task*, eds. Carl F. H. Henry and W. Stanley Mooneyham (Minneapolis: World Wide Publications, 1967), 158.

[23] Ibid., 159.

Epilogue

PROMISES MADE

More than forty years ago I was asked by a Methodist bishop, "Do you trust that you are inwardly moved by the Holy Spirit to take upon you the office of the ministry in the Church of Christ, to serve God, for the promoting of his glory and the edifying of the people?"[1]

My answer in the affirmative expressed a deep sense of calling and dedication. Later, in taking the ordination vows for the office of elder, I promised "to minister the doctrine of Christ," and in His Spirit "to defend the Church against all doctrine contrary to God's Word."[2] When admitted into full membership of the Indiana Methodist Conference in 1953, these vows were enlarged to include, among other things, a commitment to strive earnestly "to be made perfect in love in this life," and to maintain the doctrine and General Rules of the Church.[3]

I wish that I could say that I have always lived up to these expectations. But, at least, I have been mindful of the obligation, and despite my shortcomings, the vows have served to keep before me a solemn pledge to God.

Because I still hold these promises inviolate, there have been occasions when I have found myself at cross-purposes with the pronouncements and policies of my church. The conflict particularly has grown out of some libertine doctrinal innovations against which I have strongly protested. My opposition has not risen out of disloyalty, as some may assume. Quite the contrary. It is precisely because of an intense love for the church of Wesley that I, along with others, cannot support many programs that bear the official imprimatur of the denomination.

In view of the generally renegade position I have taken, frequently persons have asked me why I remain a Methodist. It is a valid question—one that a number of my friends with similar convictions have answered logically by joining the millions in my generation who have left the church. While their going diminishes the strength of the evangelical remnant who stay, I understand their feelings, and rejoice that so many of them have found more compatible fellowship in other communions. After all, John Wesley took much the same course with the ecclesiastical order of his day, though technically, despite the buffeting of the hierarchy, he remained a priest of the decadent Church of England until the end of his life.

THE SPIRIT OF WESLEY

In this sense, I, too, still have credentials with the church of my youth, though, as with Wesley, increasingly my ministry has followed the movement of the Gospel in a much wider sphere of outreach. What difference does the name on the church door make?

As to the future of United Methodism, there is cause for concern.[4] The loss of more than 2,000,000 members in the past two decades is the greatest loss in so short a period ever sustained by an American denomination. And though some leaders have expressed alarm and called for renewal,[5] by and large the cancer of theological apostasy that eats at the vitals of evangelism is not being addressed, least of all in Methodist colleges and seminaries. Until the issue is resolved with integrity, and the faith and commitment that gave birth to the Wesleyan revival recovered, we cannot expect a change of direction.

But this is no reason for despair. Whatever happens to the program of the United Methodist Church, however disturbing its loss of mission, God is not defeated. The wellsprings of evangelism are not bound by a dying institution. Methodism, as any movement raised up through the Spirit and the Word, is at heart a community of faith living under the mandate of Christ to make disciples of all nations, and in this apostolic descent, the spirit of Wesley is more alive today than ever before.

Do you not see it? You will recognize its presence in a Billy Graham Crusade as multitudes surge forward at the invitation to receive Christ; you will sense its vigor in an interdenominational neighborhood home Bible study; you will catch its witness in a Salvation Army open-air street meeting; you will understand its excitement in a Southern Baptist evangelism conference; you will find its commitment in a Campus Crusade action group; you will realize its explosive force in the mushrooming Sunday school of a growing independent church; you will know its joy in a Catholic charismatic renewal celebration; you will thrill with its vision in the hearts of thousands of young people committing themselves to world service at the triennial Urbana missions conference; and in a thousand other forms of Spirit-filled evangelism you will feel the dynamic of the Great Commission in our time. This is the Wesleyan heartbeat, the spirit of true Methodism, by whatever name it is called.

Here I find my identity—and my fellowship. Here, too, I can rejoice, confident that the ingathering of the church of Jesus Christ will increase with the years, until the work is done and the kingdom comes to fruition in the eternal praise of God.

A VICTORIOUS CHURCH

That is why the sons and daughters of Wesley live with a sparkle in their eye. The church militant will become the church triumphant. Why should we care where God places us in His service? That is His affair, not ours. And whatever our appointed work, we know that nothing can ultimately prevail against Immanuel's mission.

This has been the assurance from the beginning that

sustained that stalwart band of daring souls who rode to
their appointments with the charge of Wesley echoing in
their souls: "You have nothing to do but to save souls.
Therefore, spend and be spent in the work."[6]

And spend themselves they did! "Of the first 737
members of the Conferences to die [up to 1847], nearly half
died before they were thirty years old, [and] two-thirds
died before they had been able to render twelve years of
service."[7] True, there were some who survived the rigors
of ministry to live to a ripe old age, but most of them
"burned themselves out for God in a few years."[8] No
insurance company would ever have given them a "pre-
ferred risk" policy.

Yet whatever the adversities, they were more than
conquerors. I can hear them now as they gathered at their
Annual Conference, looking around the ragged assembly to
see who among their comrades were missing, then amid
tears of sadness and joy, lifting their voices and singing:

> And are we yet alive,
>   And see each other's face?
> Glory and praise to Jesus give,
>   For His redeeming grace.
>
> Preserved by power divine,
>   To full salvation here,
> Again in Jesus' praise we join,
>   And in His sight appear.
>
> What troubles have we seen!
>   What conflicts have we pass'd
> Fightings without, and fears within,
>   Since we assembled last!
>
> But out of all the Lord
>   Hath brought us by His love;
> And still He doth His help afford,
>   And hides our life above.
>
> Then let us make our boast
>   Of His redeeming power,

Which saves us to the uttermost,
Till we can sin no more:

Let us take up the cross,
Till we the crown obtain;
And gladly reckon all things loss,
So we may Jesus gain.[9]

AN EXAMPLE OF TRUTH

Bishop Francis Asbury was one of the few traveling ministers whose relentless labor extended over many years. But characteristic of them all, when his strength at last failed, having traveled 275,000 miles on wilderness roads, most of it on horseback, he wrote in his Journal, "Whether health, life or death, good is the will of the Lord: I will trust Him; yea, and will praise Him: He is the strength of my heart and my portion forever, Glory! Glory! Glory!"[10]

He preached his last sermon in Richmond, Virginia, on March 24, 1816. Arriving at the church, he was so weak in body that he had to be carried into the pulpit, and held up on a table by two men as he spoke. Though he had to make frequent pauses in the course of his sermon for the purpose of recovering breath, he preached for nearly an hour with great feeling on the text in Romans 9:28: "For He will finish the work, and cut it short in righteousness: because a short work will the Lord make upon the earth."

> The audience was much affected. Indeed, how could it be otherwise? To behold a venerable old man, under the dignified character of an ecclesiastical patriarch, whose silver locks indicated that time had already numbered his years, and whose palled countenance and trembling limbs presaged that his earthly race was nearly finished: to see in the mist of those melancholy signals of decaying nature, a soul beaming with immortality, and heart kindled with divine fire from the altar of God.[11]

Having delivered his testimony, the bishop was carried from the pulpit back to his carriage. He wanted to

go to Fredericksburg, but because of inclement weather
and his failing strength, after several days of traveling, he
stopped about twenty miles from town at the home of an
old friend, George Arnold.

Toward evening he became greatly indisposed. His
cough increased, and it was difficult for him to rest, finding
it impossible to lie down. Early the next morning, he
remarked that he had passed a night of much suffering and
suggested that the end was drawing near. Remembering
that it was Sunday, he requested that the family be called
into his room for worship.

What a scene that must have been! The indomitable
leader, so emaciated that he seemed more dead than alive,
was propped up in bed, while members of the household
gathered around him. They sang a hymn, someone offered
prayer, and his friend read and expounded a portion of
Scripture from Revelation 21. During the service Bishop
Asbury appeared calm and much engaged in devotion.

They offered him a little barley water, but he was
unable to swallow, and soon his speech began to fail.
Observing the obvious distress of his traveling companion,
Brother Bond, the bishop raised his hand and looked at
him peacefully. Bond leaned over and asked Asbury if he
felt the Lord Jesus to be precious to his soul. Whereupon
the valorous saint, now unable to speak, with great effort,
lifted both his hands in token of triumph. A few moments
later, without a struggle, his head slumped over, and the
old warrior entered into his rest.[12]

What a beautiful way to leave this world—with hands
lifted toward heaven, witnessing to the hosts above and to
the saints below that God is faithful who has promised and
that not one word has failed that He has spoken. In every
circumstance, His grace is sufficient.

A CHARGE TO KEEP

As the apostle Paul came to the close of his journey
and while awaiting execution, he gave to Timothy a solemn
farewell charge: "Preach the Word, be prepared in season

and out of season; correct, rebuke and encourage—with great patience and careful instruction" (2 Tim. 4:2, NIV). Knowing that false teachers would arise to turn people away from sound doctrine, he exhorted his son in the Gospel to keep his head, "endure hardship, do the work of an evangelist, discharge all the duties" of his ministry (2 Tim. 4:4–5, NIV). The way these words come together indicates a relationship between proclaiming the Word, theological integrity, suffering, bringing people to the Savior, and proving the ministry. I suspect that they always go together.

After delivering the charge, Paul concludes with his testimony: "I have fought the good fight, I have finished the race, I have kept the faith" (2 Tim. 4:7, NIV). Not a bad way to end any message. If we cannot back up what we say by our own experience, no one else is likely to take it seriously. Paul does not boast of any great church growth success nor speak of a celebrity status in opinion polls; he simply affirms his obedience to the heavenly vision. What a consolation that must be at the end of the way!

Then, knowing that soon he would give account for his works in the flesh, he rejoiced in the "crown" that "the righteous Judge" would give him in that day (2 Tim. 4:8). The word used here does not refer to a diadem worn by a king, but rather to an award for achievement, like a wreath given to an athlete for victory (e.g. 1 Cor. 9:24–25).[13] Not that we are saved by anything we do, for redemption is entirely God's work of grace. But as a believer, we start working for God. Now He gets the honor for it, though someday the saint will receive a reward. The crown speaks of that recognition for faithfulness to the mission of Christ, and as such, reflects the glory of His grace. No wonder Paul yearned for the day of his Lord's appearing.

He was not alone in that expectation. Everyone in the bonds of the Great Commission shares this longing of the soul. While it does not yet appear what we shall be, we know that when our King returns, then we shall be like him, for we shall see Him as He is, and in that day, every knee shall bow before Him, and every tongue confess to the glory of the Father, that Jesus Christ is Lord.

Until then, we have a charge to keep, a calling to fulfill. It will not be easy. But as we go forth to make disciples, we can join with Wesley in singing:

No condemnation now I dread—
Jesus, and all in him, is mine;
Alive in him, my living Head,
And clothed in righteousness divine,
Bold I approached th'eternal throne,
And claim the crown, through Christ my own.[14]

NOTES

[1] Ordination vows, "The Office of Deacons," *Discipline* (1948), 504.

[2] Ordination vows, "The Office of Elders," Ibid., 509.

[3] Vows for Admission to an Annual Conference, Ibid., 520.

[4] Though the largest numerical defection has been in mainline American Methodism, an even greater percentage of membership loss has occurred in the mother church in England. One who called attention to this deterioration earlier in the century and pleaded for renewal was W. E. Sangster in his book, *Methodism Can Be Reborn* (New York: The Methodist Book Concern, 1938). Those churchmen in his day who tried to gloss over the decline he called "shallow optimists"—persons who "mouth their bright platitudes, and rebuke us for our pessimism." Then, with indignant realism, he wrote, "They are not to be tolerated. Optimism has some superficial resemblance to Christian faith, but it has no root. It is an insufferable counterfeit: it ignores the realities of the situation: it is bland, and fiddles while Rome burns" (p. 16).

[5] Recent published expressions include Earl G. Hunt, Jr., *A Bishop Speaks His Mind* (Nashville: Abingdon, 1987); Richard B. Wilke, *And Are We Yet Alive* (Nashville: Abingdon, 1986); William H. Willimon and Robert L. Wilson, *Rekindling the Flame* (Nashville: Abingdon, 1987); James V. Heidinger II, *United Methodist Renewal: What Will It Take?* (Wilmore, Ky.: Bristol, 1988); and Ira Gallaway, *Drifted Astray* (Nashville: Abingdon, 1983). To this might be added Thomas C. Oden's *Agenda for Theology* (San Francisco: Harper & Row, 1979). The most articulate and consistent voice for renewal today in United Methodism comes through *Good News* magazine published by the Forum for Scriptural Christianity in Wilmore, Kentucky 40390.

[6] John Wesley, *Minutes of Several Conversations, Works*, 8:310.

[7] Halford E. Luccock and Paul Hutchinson, p. 229.

[8] Ibid., 230.

[9] From Charles Wesley's hymn, "And Are We Yet Alive?" This hymn was sung at the beginning of every early Methodist Annual Conference, a practice that still persists in most conferences today.

[10] Asbury, *Journal and Letters*, 2:794.

[11] Francis Holingsworth, "A Short Account of His Death," Ibid., 802.

[12] The complete account is in Ibid., 801–804. For a moving remembrance of Bishop Asbury by his traveling companion at the time of his death, read "John Wesley Bond's Reminiscences of Francis Asbury," in Norwood, *Sourcebook of American Methodism*, 34–40.

[13] For a comprehensive treatment of these terms, see Gerhard Kittel and Gerhard Friedrick, eds., *Theological Dictionary of the New Testament*, 10 vols. (Grand Rapids: Eerdmans, 1970), 7:615–36.

[14] Charles Wesley, from the hymn "And Can It Be."